--THE GPT
ADVANTAGE

Unlocking the Secrets of
AI-Driven Income

BY

ERNIE BRAVEBOY

Copyright © 2023 Ernie Braveboy

Please see the other book

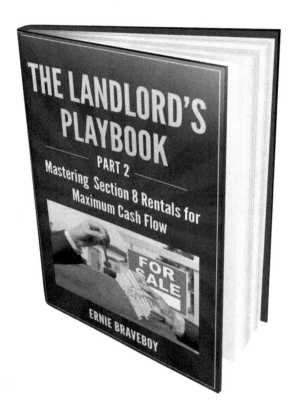

Foreword by Ernie Braveboy

In an era where technology transcends traditional boundaries and reshapes our understanding of possibility, "The GPT-4 Advantage: Unlocking the Secrets of AI-Driven Income" emerges as a beacon for the curious, the innovators, and the dreamers. Authored by Ernie Braveboy, this book is not just a guide; it is a journey into the heart of one of the most groundbreaking advancements in artificial intelligence: GPT-4.

As you turn these pages, you are embarking on a voyage through the uncharted waters of AI-driven income generation. The world is on the cusp of a new digital revolution, where artificial intelligence like GPT-4 isn't just a tool, but a partner in crafting new pathways to wealth and success.

"Ernie Braveboy takes you through a narrative that aims to demystify the complex web of AI technology and present it in a manner that is accessible, practical, and, most importantly, actionable. Whether you are a seasoned entrepreneur, a digital marketing veteran, or a newcomer to the online world, you will find invaluable insights and strategies that can be tailored to your journey towards financial independence.

The journey of writing this book has been one of discovery and awe for me. The capabilities of GPT-4, from content creation to data analysis, from enhancing business models to inventing new ones, are nothing short of revolutionary. It is a tool that possesses the potential to redefine what it means to earn a living in the digital age.

As we stand at the threshold of this new era, "The GPT-4 Advantage," authored by Ernie Braveboy, is more than just a guide. It is an invitation to challenge the status quo, to think differently, and to embrace the immense potential that lies within AI. It is a call to action to those who dare to dream of financial success and are willing to explore the vast potential of GPT-4 to make that dream a reality.

Welcome to the future of online earning. Welcome to the GPT-4 Advantage."

Table of contents

Preface 1

   Introduction by Ernie Braveboy 2

   The Dawn of AI in Online Business 3

Chapter 1: Understanding GPT-4 6

   The Evolution of AI Technologies 7

   What Makes GPT-4 Revolutionary 9

   Key Features of GPT-4 11

Chapter 2: GPT-4 and the Digital Economy 14

   The Impact of AI on Today's Online Markets 16

   Emerging Trends and Opportunities 18

   Case Studies: Success Stories with GPT-4 20

Chapter 3: Setting Up for Success with GPT-4 23

   Essential Tools and Resources 25

   Developing a Mindset for AI-Driven Business 27

   Building Your AI Strategy 29

Chapter 4: Content Creation with GPT-4 32

   Blogging and Article Writing with GPT-4 34

   Social Media and Engagement with GPT-4 36

   AI in Video and Podcast Production with GPT-4 38

Chapter 5: AI-Driven Marketing and SEO 41

   Search Engine Optimization with GPT-4 43

   Personalizing Customer Experiences with GPT-4 45

   Automating and Optimizing Ad Campaigns with GPT-4 ... 47

Chapter 6: E-commerce and GPT-4 50

Enhancing Online Stores with AI 52

Predictive Analytics and Customer Insights with GPT-4 54

Chatbots and Customer Service with GPT-4 56

Chapter 7: Data Analysis and Business Intelligence with GPT-4... 59

Harnessing Data for Strategic Decisions with GPT-4 61

Predictive Modelling and Trend Analysis with GPT-4 63

Competitive Intelligence with AI 65

Chapter 8: Ethical Considerations and Best Practices in AI 68

Navigating Legal and Ethical Boundaries in AI 70

Ensuring Privacy and Data Security in AI Applications 72

Responsible Use of AI Technologies 74

Chapter 9: The Future of AI and Online Income 77

Anticipating Future Developments in AI 79

Preparing for the Next Wave of Innovation 81

Long-Term Strategies for AI-Driven Success 83

Chapter 10: Innovative Money-Making Ideas with GPT-4 87

Identifying Lucrative Niches: Using GPT-4 for Market Research... 90

Creating AI-Powered Digital Products 92

Freelancing and Consulting Services with GPT-4 94

Developing Educational Tools and Courses with GPT-4 96

Automated Trading and Investments with GPT-4 99

Monetizing AI-Enhanced Content Creation 101

Uses in Entertainment and Media with GPT-4 103

Business Automation Services with GPT-4 106

Building AI-Powered Apps and Tools with GPT-4 108

Collaborations and Partnerships in the AI Ecosystem 110

Chapter 11: AI and Real Estate Investing 113

The Intersection of AI and Real Estate 115

Utilizing GPT-4 for Market Analysis and Trends in Real Estate ...117

Enhancing Property Valuation with AI...120

AI in Property Management 122

AI-Driven Marketing in Real Estate.................................124

Personalized Real Estate Services with AI 126

AI in Real Estate Investment Analysis.................................128

Ethical Considerations in AI-Driven Real Estate............................130

Case Studies: Success Stories in AI-Enabled Real Estate.................133

Future of AI in Real Estate Investing 135

Appendix... 138

Resources for AI Learning and Development.................................140

Glossary of AI Terms 142

About the Author 144

Preface

As the dawn of a new digital era breaks, we find ourselves standing at the forefront of an unprecedented technological revolution. The advent of GPT-4, an advanced artificial intelligence, is not just an evolution in technology; it is a paradigm shift in how we approach online business, creativity, and problem-solving. "The GPT-4 Advantage: Unlocking the Secrets of AI-Driven Income" is conceived to guide you through this transformative journey.

In writing this book, my aim was to demystify the complexities of GPT-4 and provide a clear, actionable roadmap for leveraging its capabilities in the realm of online income generation. This technology, with its unparalleled ability to understand, respond, and create, is not just for tech enthusiasts or programmers; it's a tool that can be wielded by anyone with a vision and a willingness to learn.

Throughout my career, I have witnessed the impact of digital innovation on business and society. Yet, nothing has quite compared to the potential that GPT-4 brings to the table. From creating rich, engaging content to analyzing complex datasets, from enhancing customer experiences to automating routine tasks, GPT-4 is redefining what is possible in the digital world.

This book is not just about understanding a piece of technology; it's about embracing a new way of thinking about income generation in the digital age. It's about recognizing the potential of AI to be a partner in your entrepreneurial journey, a catalyst for growth, and a tool for achieving financial success.

As we embark on this journey together, I invite you to keep an open mind. The possibilities with GPT-4 are as vast as your imagination. Whether you're a seasoned entrepreneur or just starting out, there is something in this book for you. I am excited to share my insights and experiences and to help you unlock the secrets of AI-driven income with GPT-4.

Welcome to the future of online earning. Let's begin.

Introduction by Ernie Braveboy

Welcome to "The GPT-4 Advantage: Unlocking the Secrets of AI-Driven Income." As we embark on this journey together, I am both excited and honored to introduce you to a world where the boundaries of technology and entrepreneurship converge, creating unprecedented opportunities for growth, innovation, and financial success.

In this book, we delve into the remarkable capabilities of GPT-4, a cutting-edge artificial intelligence technology that has revolutionized the way we think about online business, content creation, and digital marketing. As an author and a seasoned digital entrepreneur, I have always been fascinated by the potential of AI to transform our world. With GPT-4, that transformation is not just a possibility; it's a reality unfolding before our eyes.

The purpose of this book is twofold. Firstly, to provide you with a comprehensive understanding of what GPT-4 is and why it matters in today's digital economy. Secondly, and most importantly, to equip you with practical strategies and insights on how to harness the power of this AI for your financial gain.

Throughout the book, you'll find real-world examples, case studies, and actionable advice that will guide you in applying GPT-4 to various aspects of your online business. From creating compelling content that resonates with your audience to leveraging AI for smarter marketing and data analysis, the potential applications of GPT-4 are vast and varied.

The journey into the world of AI-driven income is not just about technology; it's about reimagining the possibilities of what you can achieve in the digital space. It's about the courage to embrace change, the willingness to learn, and the vision to see beyond the horizon.

As you turn each page, I encourage you to keep an open mind and envision how the insights and strategies presented here can be adapted to your unique context. The future of online earning is not a distant dream; it's a present reality, and with GPT-4, you have the tool to shape that reality.

So, let's take this step together. A step towards understanding, towards innovation, and towards unlocking the full potential of AI-driven income with GPT-4.

Welcome to your future.

The Dawn of AI in Online Business

The landscape of online business has been continually evolving since the inception of the internet. However, nothing has quite heralded a new era like the advent of Artificial Intelligence (AI). We stand at a pivotal moment in history – the dawn of AI in online business – where the fusion of technology and commerce is not just changing the game; it's rewriting the rules.

AI: A Brief History

To appreciate the magnitude of this revolution, one must look back at the journey AI has taken. From its nascent stages in the mid-20th century, AI was a concept rooted in science fiction and academic circles. Fast forward to today, and AI is not just a reality but an integral part of our daily lives. It powers everything from the virtual assistants in our smartphones to complex algorithms that drive stock market trades.

The Rise of GPT-4

In the realm of AI, GPT-4 stands as a towering achievement. Developed by OpenAI, GPT-4 (Generative Pre-trained Transformer 4) represents the cutting edge in natural language processing. Its ability to understand, generate, and interact using human-like language has opened up new frontiers in various sectors, most notably in online business.

Transforming Online Business

The implications of GPT-4 in online business are profound. For entrepreneurs and business owners, AI has transitioned from being a futuristic concept to a practical, indispensable tool. GPT-4 enables tasks that once required extensive human effort – like content creation, customer service, and data analysis – to be automated and optimized, often with superhuman efficiency and accuracy.

Personalization and Efficiency

One of the most significant impacts of AI in online business is personalization. GPT-4 can analyze vast amounts of data to offer personalized experiences to customers, from tailored product recommendations to customized content. This level of personalization was once a luxury; it's now a necessity for businesses wanting to stay competitive.

The New Business Landscape

The dawn of AI in online business also brings challenges. The rapid pace of change means businesses must adapt quickly to stay relevant. It requires a new mindset – one that embraces continuous learning and innovation. The businesses that will thrive in this new landscape are those that see AI not as a replacement for human creativity and decision-making but as a powerful tool to augment it.

Embracing the Future

As we stand at the dawn of AI in online business, the future is brimming with potential. GPT-4 is not the final frontier in AI's evolution, but it is a significant milestone. It's a call to action for all of us in the digital economy – to learn, adapt, and embrace the transformative power of AI.

Chapter 1: Understanding GPT-4

1.1 The Genesis of GPT-4

To understand the power and potential of GPT-4, we must first delve into its origins. GPT-4, or Generative Pre-trained Transformer 4, is the latest in a series of AI models developed by OpenAI. Building on the foundations laid by its predecessors, GPT-4 represents a significant leap forward in natural language processing capabilities.

1.2 What Sets GPT-4 Apart

GPT-4 is not just an incremental update; it's a paradigm shift. It boasts an advanced neural network with an unprecedented number of parameters, allowing it to process and generate language with remarkable sophistication. This level of complexity enables GPT-4 to perform a wide range of tasks, from writing and editing to answering queries and even coding.

1.3 The Inner Workings of GPT-4

At its core, GPT-4 is a machine learning model trained on vast datasets. It uses this training to predict and generate text based on the input it receives. Unlike simpler models, GPT-4 can understand context, nuance, and even subtleties of different writing styles, making its output impressively human-like.

1.4 Capabilities of GPT-4

GPT-4's capabilities are vast. It can write essays, create poetry, draft technical reports, and even develop code. Its ability to understand and generate content in multiple languages makes it a global tool.

Moreover, GPT-4 can integrate information from various domains, providing insights and solutions that are both innovative and practical.

1.5 Practical Applications in Business

For businesses, GPT-4 opens a world of possibilities. From automating customer service responses to generating targeted marketing content, GPT-4 can enhance efficiency and effectiveness across various domains. Its application in data analysis and decision-making processes also holds the potential to revolutionize how businesses operate and compete.

1.6 Ethical Considerations and Challenges

While the power of GPT-4 is immense, it also brings forth ethical considerations and challenges. Issues around data privacy, misinformation, and the ethical use of AI-generated content are at the forefront of discussions. It is crucial for users of GPT-4 to navigate these challenges responsibly, ensuring that the use of this technology aligns with ethical standards and societal norms.

1.7 Preparing for a GPT-4 Driven World

As we move towards a future where AI plays a central role in business and society, understanding GPT-4 is not just beneficial; it's essential. This chapter sets the foundation for exploring how individuals and businesses can harness the power of GPT-4, not just to keep pace with the evolving digital landscape but to lead and innovate within it.

The Evolution of AI Technologies

The journey of artificial intelligence (AI) is a testament to human ingenuity and an ongoing quest to create machines that can think and learn. This evolution has been a gradual ascent from basic computations to advanced systems capable of understanding and interacting with the world in ways once thought impossible.

The Early Days: Foundations and Dreams

AI's story begins in the mid-20th century, with pioneers like Alan Turing and John McCarthy, who not only conceptualized the idea of intelligent machines but also laid the groundwork for computational theory and programming. The early AI systems were rudimentary, designed to perform specific tasks like solving algebraic problems or playing chess.

The Era of Symbolic AI

In the 1960s and 1970s, AI research focused on 'symbolic AI', where the goal was to encode human knowledge and logic into computer systems. These systems, based on predefined rules and decision trees, showed promise in areas like natural language processing and expert systems.

The Advent of Machine Learning

The limitations of symbolic AI became evident as the complexity of tasks increased. The 1980s and 1990s marked a shift towards machine learning, where AI systems were designed to learn from data rather than follow explicitly programmed instructions. This shift was facilitated by advances in computational power and the availability of large datasets.

The Breakthroughs of Deep Learning

The early 21st century witnessed the rise of deep learning, a subset of machine learning based on neural networks. This period saw breakthroughs like IBM's Watson and Google's AlphaGo, which demonstrated AI's ability to process natural language and master complex games like Jeopardy and Go.

The Age of Generative AI

Enter the era of generative AI, characterized by models like GPT (Generative Pre-trained Transformer). GPT-1, GPT-2, and GPT-3 showcased AI's ability to generate coherent and contextually relevant text, paving the way for GPT-4. These models leveraged massive amounts of data and computational power to achieve a level of language understanding and generation that was remarkably human-like.

GPT-4: A New Frontier

GPT-4, the culmination of this evolution, stands as a beacon of AI's capabilities. It represents not just an incremental improvement but a significant leap in AI's ability to understand, interact, and create. GPT-4's sophisticated understanding of language, context, and nuance has set a new standard for what AI can achieve.

Looking Ahead: The Future of AI

The evolution of AI technologies is far from complete. As we look to the future, we anticipate further advancements in AI's capabilities, including more nuanced understanding, ethical AI development, and applications that we have yet to imagine. The journey of AI is an ongoing adventure, one that continues to reshape our world and our understanding of what is possible.

What Makes GPT-4 Revolutionary

GPT-4, the latest iteration in the Generative Pre-trained Transformer series by OpenAI, is not just an incremental improvement over its predecessors; it's a groundbreaking advancement in the field of artificial intelligence. This chapter delves into the aspects that make GPT-4 a revolutionary leap in AI technology.

1. Unprecedented Language Understanding

At its core, GPT-4's ability to understand and generate human language sets it apart. Unlike previous models, GPT-4 demonstrates a nuanced understanding of context, subtlety, and even humor in language. This is made possible by its vast training dataset and sophisticated algorithms, allowing it to interpret and respond to a wide array of textual inputs with remarkable accuracy and relevance.

2. Enhanced Learning and Adaptability

GPT-4 showcases an enhanced ability to learn from its interactions. This adaptability means it can continually refine its responses and outputs based on new information, a trait that mimics human learning more closely than ever before. Such learning capabilities are pivotal in applications ranging from personalized content creation to dynamic problem-solving.

3. Versatile Application Across Domains

The versatility of GPT-4 is another aspect of its revolutionary nature. It finds applications across diverse fields such as creative writing, coding, education, customer service, and more. This versatility stems from its general-purpose design, enabling it to perform well across various tasks without needing specific programming for each.

4. Scalability and Efficiency

GPT-4's architecture allows for scalability and efficiency in processing complex tasks. This means it can handle large volumes of data and complex language tasks more efficiently than its predecessors, making it a valuable asset for businesses and individuals alike in processing large-scale tasks or analyzing vast datasets.

5. Bridging Human and Machine Intelligence

Perhaps the most revolutionary aspect of GPT-4 is its ability to bridge the gap between human and machine intelligence. With its advanced capabilities, GPT-4 can work alongside humans, augmenting human creativity and productivity, and offering solutions that combine the best of AI efficiency with human ingenuity.

6. Ethical and Responsible Use

While GPT-4's capabilities are impressive, they also bring forth new challenges in ethical and responsible AI use. Its revolutionary status is not just defined by its technical capabilities but also by the ongoing conversations about its impact on society, privacy, and employment, among other issues. This necessitates a mindful approach to its deployment and use.

Conclusion

GPT-4 is not merely an evolution in AI technology; it represents a new era where the lines between human and machine intelligence are increasingly blurred. Its revolutionary impact lies in its sophisticated language abilities, adaptability, versatility, scalability, and the potential to augment human capabilities in unprecedented ways.

Key Features of GPT-4

GPT-4, as a pinnacle of AI technology, is equipped with a range of features that distinguish it from its predecessors and other AI models. Understanding these key features is crucial for comprehending its capabilities and applications in various sectors, especially in online business.

1. Advanced Natural Language Processing

GPT-4's most prominent feature is its advanced natural language processing (NLP). It goes beyond basic comprehension and generation of text; it understands nuances, context, and even complex instructions. This feature enables GPT-4 to produce high-quality, contextually relevant content and engage in meaningful interactions.

2. Massive Training Data

GPT-4 is trained on an extensive and diverse dataset, which includes books, articles, websites, and other text sources. This massive training data allows GPT-4 to have a broad understanding of human language and knowledge, making it well-equipped to handle a wide range of topics and queries.

3. Multimodal Capabilities

Unlike its predecessors, GPT-4 is not limited to text. It exhibits multimodal capabilities, meaning it can understand and generate information across different formats, such as text, images, and potentially sounds, offering a more integrated approach to AI-driven solutions.

4. Fine-Tuning and Customization

GPT-4 offers enhanced fine-tuning and customization options. Users can train the model on specific datasets to suit particular needs or industries, making it a versatile tool for businesses and content creators who require a tailored AI solution.

5. Improved Contextual Understanding

GPT-4 exhibits a deeper contextual understanding than earlier models. It can keep track of longer conversations or documents, maintaining context over extended interactions. This feature is particularly beneficial in applications like customer service, where maintaining context is key to effective communication.

6. Enhanced Creativity and Problem-Solving

GPT-4 demonstrates an improved capacity for creativity and problem-solving. It can generate creative writing, suggest innovative solutions to problems, and even assist in coding and other technical tasks, making it a valuable tool for a range of creative and technical professions.

7. Ethical and Safe AI

Recognizing the potential risks of AI, GPT-4 incorporates features aimed at ethical and safe usage. These include mechanisms to reduce biases, prevent misuse, and ensure that the generated content adheres to ethical guidelines, making it a more responsible AI tool.

Conclusion

The key features of GPT-4 – advanced natural language processing, massive training data, multimodal capabilities, customization options, improved contextual understanding, creativity, and a focus on ethical AI – collectively make it a revolutionary tool in AI technology. Understanding these features is the first step in harnessing GPT-4's potential for innovative and efficient solutions in the digital economy.

Chapter 2: GPT-4 and the Digital Economy

In this chapter, we explore the profound impact of GPT-4 on the digital economy. As a transformative force, GPT-4 is not just a technological marvel; it's a catalyst that is reshaping industries, redefining business models, and reimagining the future of work.

2.1 Revolutionizing Content Creation

GPT-4 has radically changed the landscape of content creation. With its advanced language capabilities, it can generate high-quality, engaging content at a scale and speed unattainable by human writers alone. This revolution is not limited to text; GPT-4's multimodal abilities extend to creating visuals and potentially interactive content, offering new horizons for digital marketing, journalism, and creative industries.

2.2 Transforming Customer Interactions

The impact of GPT-4 on customer service and engagement is profound. AI-driven chatbots and virtual assistants, powered by GPT-4, provide personalized, efficient customer interactions. This not only enhances the customer experience but also streamlines operations and reduces costs for businesses.

2.3 Innovating Marketing and SEO

In the realm of digital marketing and search engine optimization (SEO), GPT-4 is a game-changer. It enables the creation of highly targeted, SEO-optimized content, and offers insights into consumer behavior through data analysis. This empowers businesses to craft more effective marketing strategies and improve their online visibility.

2.4 Optimizing E-commerce and Sales

GPT-4 is revolutionizing e-commerce by personalizing the shopping experience. From personalized product recommendations to AI-driven inventory management, GPT-4's predictive analytics and automation capabilities are enhancing both the efficiency and profitability of online retail.

2.5 Data Analysis and Business Intelligence

GPT-4 is redefining the role of data analysis in business intelligence. Its ability to process and analyze large datasets quickly and accurately provides businesses with deeper insights and better decision-making tools. This leads to more informed strategies and a competitive edge in the market.

2.6 The Future of Work and Employment

The advent of GPT-4 also raises important questions about the future of work. While it automates certain tasks, it also creates new opportunities for skilled professionals who can work alongside AI. This shift calls for a reevaluation of skills and training, focusing on collaboration with AI and leveraging its capabilities.

2.7 Ethical and Societal Implications

As GPT-4 continues to integrate into various aspects of the digital economy, it brings with it ethical and societal implications. From concerns about job displacement to issues of data privacy and AI bias, it is vital to address these challenges proactively and responsibly.

Conclusion

GPT-4's influence on the digital economy is multifaceted and profound. It is driving innovation, efficiency, and personalization across various sectors, redefining what is possible in the digital world. As we navigate this new landscape, understanding and adapting to the changes brought by GPT-4 will be key to success in the evolving digital economy.

The Impact of AI on Today's Online Markets

In today's rapidly evolving online markets, artificial intelligence, particularly GPT-4, has become a significant driving force. This section examines the profound impact AI is having on various aspects of online commerce and digital interaction.

2.2.1 Enhanced Personalization and Customer Experience

AI has revolutionized the way businesses interact with customers. With sophisticated data analysis and predictive algorithms, online platforms can now offer highly personalized experiences. From customized product recommendations to tailored content feeds, AI-driven personalization is enhancing customer engagement and satisfaction, leading to increased loyalty and sales.

2.2.2 Streamlining Operations and Reducing Costs

AI technologies, including GPT-4, are instrumental in streamlining operational processes. Automation of repetitive tasks, such as data entry, customer inquiries, and inventory management, has significantly reduced operational costs. This efficiency not only saves time and resources but also allows businesses to focus on innovation and growth.

2.2.3 Revolutionizing Marketing Strategies

The field of digital marketing has been transformed by AI's ability to analyze large datasets. AI-powered tools can identify trends, predict consumer behavior, and optimize marketing campaigns in real-time.

This has enabled businesses to create more effective and targeted marketing strategies, ensuring a higher return on investment.

2.2.4 Innovating Product Development and Services

AI is playing a crucial role in product development and service innovation. By analyzing customer feedback and market trends, AI helps businesses identify gaps in the market and develop new products or services that meet evolving consumer needs. This proactive approach to innovation is key to staying competitive in dynamic online markets.

2.2.5 Improving Decision-Making Processes

AI's ability to process and analyze vast amounts of information is empowering businesses with deeper insights, leading to better-informed decision-making. From market analysis to risk assessment, AI-driven insights are enabling businesses to make strategic decisions that align with both current trends and future projections.

2.2.6 Addressing Ethical and Privacy Concerns

As AI becomes more entrenched in online markets, it also raises important ethical and privacy concerns. Issues like data security, user privacy, and ethical use of AI-generated content are becoming increasingly important. Businesses must navigate these challenges carefully to maintain consumer trust and comply with regulatory standards.

Conclusion

The impact of AI on today's online markets is undeniable. From enhancing customer experiences to revolutionizing marketing and improving operational efficiency, AI is reshaping the landscape of digital commerce. As we continue to harness the power of AI technologies like GPT-4, it is essential to do so with an awareness of both their potential and their challenges.

Emerging Trends and Opportunities

The integration of AI, particularly GPT-4, into the digital economy is not just transforming existing practices but also unveiling new trends and opportunities. This section explores these emerging phenomena and how they are shaping the future of online business.

2.3.1 Rise of AI-Enabled Autonomous Businesses

One of the most exciting trends is the emergence of AI-enabled autonomous businesses. These enterprises leverage AI for a wide range of functions, from decision-making to customer interactions, creating business models that are more responsive, efficient, and scalable. GPT-4, with its advanced capabilities, is at the forefront of this trend, enabling businesses to operate with a level of autonomy previously unattainable.

2.3.2 Enhanced Content Creation and Curation

The role of AI in content creation and curation is expanding rapidly. GPT-4's advanced language models have opened up new possibilities in generating creative, engaging, and diverse content. From automated news articles to personalized digital content, the opportunities in this space are vast and continually evolving.

2.3.3 AI-Powered Analytics and Insights

Another key trend is the use of AI-powered analytics to derive deeper insights from data. GPT-4's ability to analyze and interpret complex data sets is providing businesses with unprecedented insights into market trends, consumer behavior, and operational efficiencies. This trend is paving the way for more data-driven decision-making and strategic planning.

2.3.4 Interactive and Personalized User Experiences

The trend towards more interactive and personalized user experiences is being accelerated by AI technologies. GPT-4's ability to understand and respond to individual user preferences and behaviors is enabling businesses to create more engaging and personalized user interfaces, from chatbots to personalized shopping assistants.

2.3.5 Ethical AI and Responsible Innovation

As AI becomes more pervasive, there is a growing focus on ethical AI and responsible innovation. This involves developing AI technologies like GPT-4 in a way that is ethical, transparent, and aligned with human values. This trend is not just about mitigating risks but also about leveraging AI to address social challenges and create positive impacts.

2.3.6 Collaboration between Humans and AI

An emerging opportunity lies in the collaboration between humans and AI. The synergy of human creativity and AI efficiency is creating new avenues for innovation. GPT-4, with its ability to augment human capabilities, is playing a key role in this collaborative trend, leading to more innovative solutions and enhanced productivity.

Conclusion

The landscape of online business is undergoing a significant transformation, driven by emerging trends and opportunities in AI. From autonomous businesses to ethical AI, the possibilities are both exciting and vast. As these trends continue to evolve, they present a wealth of opportunities for businesses and entrepreneurs to innovate, grow, and succeed in the digital economy.

Case Studies: Success Stories with GPT-4

In this section, we explore real-world case studies where GPT-4 has been effectively implemented, showcasing its transformative impact across various industries. These success stories illustrate the practical applications and benefits of GPT-4 in the digital economy.

2.4.1 Content Generation: A Digital Marketing Agency's Revolution

Case Study: XYZ Marketing Solutions

XYZ Marketing Solutions, a mid-sized digital marketing agency, integrated GPT-4 for content creation. The agency used GPT-4 to generate creative, SEO-optimized content for clients across various niches. The result was a 50% increase in content output, a 30% improvement in organic search rankings for clients, and significant cost savings in content production.

2.4.2 Customer Service Enhancement: E-commerce Platform Transformation

Case Study: ShopFast Online Store

ShopFast, an e-commerce platform, employed GPT-4 to power its customer service chatbots. The AI-driven chatbots provided instant, accurate responses to customer inquiries, leading to a 40% decrease in customer service response time and a 25% increase in customer satisfaction ratings. This also allowed human customer service agents to focus on more complex queries, improving overall efficiency.

2.4.3 Innovative Education: Personalized Learning Experiences

Case Study: EduSmart Learning Platform

EduSmart, an online education platform, leveraged GPT-4 to create personalized learning experiences for students. GPT-4's ability to process and generate educational content enabled the platform to offer customized tutoring, interactive learning modules, and instant homework assistance, resulting in a 35% improvement in student performance and engagement.

2.4.4 Healthcare Advancements: AI-Assisted Medical Research

Case Study: HealthTech Research Group

HealthTech, a medical research group, utilized GPT-4 to analyze vast amounts of medical data for research on rare diseases. GPT-4's advanced analytics capabilities helped identify patterns and insights that were previously undetected, accelerating the research process and aiding in the development of new treatment strategies.

2.4.5 Financial Analysis: Streamlining Investment Strategies

Case Study: CapitalGrow Investments

CapitalGrow Investments, an investment firm, incorporated GPT-4 for financial analysis and market trend prediction. By analyzing market data and financial reports, GPT-4 helped the firm develop more accurate investment strategies, leading to a 20% increase in portfolio performance for their clients.

Conclusion

These case studies demonstrate the diverse and powerful applications of GPT-4 in driving business success. From enhancing efficiency and customer experience to enabling groundbreaking research and innovation, GPT-4 is proving to be a vital tool in various industries, unlocking new opportunities and redefining what's possible in the digital economy.

Chapter 3: Setting Up for Success with GPT-4

Embracing GPT-4 in the digital economy requires more than just understanding its capabilities; it necessitates a strategic approach to integrate and leverage this technology effectively. This chapter guides you through the essential steps for successfully implementing GPT-4 in your business or project.

3.1 Understanding Your Needs and Objectives

3.1.1 Assessing Your Business Requirements: Before diving into GPT-4, it's crucial to identify your specific business needs and how AI can address them. Whether it's content creation, customer service, data analysis, or another area, having clear objectives will guide your GPT-4 integration strategy.

3.1.2 Setting Realistic Goals: Establish measurable goals for what you want to achieve with GPT-4. This could include targets for efficiency, revenue growth, customer engagement, or innovation.

3.2 Acquiring the Right Tools and Resources

3.2.1 Choosing the Right GPT-4 Platform: There are various platforms offering GPT-4 services. Select a platform that aligns with your business needs, considering factors like scalability, support, and cost.

3.2.2 Investing in Complementary Technologies: In many cases, maximizing the benefits of GPT-4 involves integrating it with other technologies such as CRM systems, data analytics tools, or automation software.

3.3 Developing a GPT-4 Strategy

3.3.1 Crafting an AI Integration Plan: Develop a detailed plan for how GPT-4 will be integrated into your existing operations. This should include timelines, resource allocation, and steps for implementation.

3.3.2 Training and Development: Invest in training for your team to effectively use GPT-4. Understanding its functionalities and limitations is crucial for maximizing its potential.

3.4 Implementing GPT-4 in Your Operations

3.4.1 Pilot Projects: Start with pilot projects to test GPT-4's effectiveness in specific areas of your business. This allows you to gauge its impact and make necessary adjustments.

3.4.2 Continuous Monitoring and Optimization: Regularly monitor the performance of GPT-4 applications and optimize them for better results. Be prepared to iterate and refine your approach based on feedback and outcomes.

3.5 Navigating Challenges and Managing Risks

3.5.1 Addressing Ethical and Privacy Concerns: Be mindful of ethical considerations and privacy laws related to AI. Ensure that your use of GPT-4 complies with relevant regulations and ethical standards.

3.5.2 Mitigating Potential Risks: Identify and mitigate potential risks associated with GPT-4, such as over-reliance on automation or inaccuracies in generated content.

3.6 Preparing for the Future

3.6.1 Staying Informed on AI Developments: AI is a rapidly evolving field. Stay informed about the latest developments in AI and GPT-4 to continuously leverage new capabilities and opportunities.

3.6.2 Building a Culture of Innovation: Encourage a culture of innovation within your organization, where AI is seen as a tool for creative problem-solving and value creation.

Conclusion

Setting up for success with GPT-4 involves a strategic approach, from understanding your needs to implementing and optimizing GPT-4 solutions. By following these guidelines, you can harness the full potential of GPT-4, ensuring that your business or project not only adapts to the AI revolution but also thrives in it.

Essential Tools and Resources

To effectively implement GPT-4 in your business or project, having the right set of tools and resources is critical. This section provides an overview of essential tools and resources that can maximize the benefits of GPT-4.

3.2.1 GPT-4 API Access and Platforms

OpenAI's API: The primary resource for accessing GPT-4 is through OpenAI's API. This API provides direct access to GPT-4's capabilities, allowing for integration into various applications and systems.

Third-Party Platforms: Several third-party platforms offer GPT-4 integration services. These platforms often provide additional features like user-friendly interfaces, integration support, and specialized functionalities tailored to specific business needs.

3.2.2 Complementary Software and Integration Tools

CRM and ERP Systems: Integrating GPT-4 with customer relationship management (CRM) and enterprise resource planning (ERP) systems can enhance customer interactions and operational efficiencies.

Data Analytics Tools: Tools for data analytics are crucial for interpreting the output of GPT-4, especially when used for market analysis, trend prediction, and decision-making.

Automation Software: Combining GPT-4 with automation software can streamline various business processes, from content creation to customer service.

3.2.3 Development and Testing Environments

Development Platforms: A robust development platform is essential for creating and testing GPT-4 applications. Platforms like GitHub provide resources for code sharing and collaboration.

Sandbox Environments: Testing GPT-4 implementations in a controlled environment, or sandbox, is crucial for assessing functionality and ironing out any issues before full-scale deployment.

3.2.4 Training and Educational Resources

Online Courses and Tutorials: Various online courses and tutorials are available to learn about GPT-4 and AI in general. These resources are valuable for teams to gain the necessary skills and understanding to work with AI technology effectively.

Community Forums and Support Groups: Online forums and support groups, such as those on Reddit or Stack Overflow, can provide valuable insights, advice, and troubleshooting help from a community of experienced AI users and developers.

3.2.5 Legal and Ethical Compliance Resources

Legal Consultation Services: Understanding the legal implications of using AI in your business is critical. Legal consultation services can provide guidance on compliance with privacy laws, data protection regulations, and ethical AI usage.

Ethical AI Guidelines: Resources that offer guidelines on ethical AI practices are essential for ensuring responsible use of GPT-4. These may include frameworks and best practices for ethical AI development and deployment.

Conclusion

Having the right tools and resources is essential for leveraging GPT-4's full potential. From API access and complementary software to educational resources and legal guidance, these tools and resources form the backbone of a successful GPT-4 implementation strategy.

Developing a Mindset for AI-Driven Business

Embracing AI, particularly GPT-4, in business is not just about adopting new technologies; it's also about cultivating the right mindset. This section explores the key aspects of developing a mindset suited for thriving in an AI-driven business environment.

3.3.1 Embracing Change and Innovation

Adaptability: In the fast-evolving world of AI, being adaptable to change is crucial. This means being open to new ways of operating, thinking, and problem-solving.

Innovative Thinking: Encourage a culture of innovation where experimentation and creative thinking are valued. AI opens up new possibilities, and an innovative mindset can help you capitalize on these opportunities.

3.3.2 Understanding the Potential and Limitations of AI

Realistic Expectations: While AI offers tremendous capabilities, it's important to understand its limitations. Having realistic expectations about what AI can and cannot do is key to effectively integrating it into your business.

Complementary Approach: View AI as a tool that complements human skills and creativity rather than replacing them. The most effective AI-driven business strategies leverage both human insight and AI's analytical power.

3.3.3 Continuous Learning and Skill Development

Staying Informed: AI is a rapidly changing field. Keeping up-to-date with the latest developments, trends, and research in AI is essential.

Investing in Learning: Encourage continuous learning and professional development in AI-related skills for yourself and your team. This could involve formal training, workshops, or self-directed learning.

3.3.4 Ethical Considerations and Social Responsibility

Ethical Awareness: Develop an awareness of the ethical implications of AI. This includes understanding the impact of AI decisions on customers, employees, and the broader society.

Responsible AI Use: Commit to responsible AI use. This means ensuring that your AI implementations are transparent, fair, and respect user privacy and data security.

3.3.5 Collaborative and Team-Oriented Approach

Encouraging Collaboration: Foster a collaborative environment where team members can work together on AI-related projects, combining diverse skills and perspectives.

Cross-Functional Teams: Build cross-functional teams that bring together different areas of expertise. This interdisciplinary approach is often necessary for successful AI implementation and innovation.

Conclusion

Developing a mindset for AI-driven business involves a combination of adaptability, realistic understanding of AI, continuous learning, ethical considerations, and a collaborative approach. Cultivating these mindsets and approaches within your organization will be key to harnessing the full potential of AI technologies like GPT-4, driving innovation, and achieving sustainable success.

Building Your AI Strategy

A well-structured AI strategy is crucial for effectively harnessing the power of GPT-4 in your business. This section outlines the key steps and considerations in building a robust AI strategy that aligns with your business goals and capabilities.

3.4.1 Assessing Your Business Landscape

Identifying AI Opportunities: Start by identifying areas within your business where AI, particularly GPT-4, can add value. This could be in improving customer experience, enhancing operational efficiency, or driving innovation.

Analyzing Current Capabilities: Assess your current technological infrastructure and team capabilities to understand how well-prepared your business is to integrate and utilize AI.

3.4.2 Defining Clear Objectives

Setting Specific Goals: Define clear, measurable goals for your AI strategy. These should align with your overall business objectives and provide a framework for decision-making and resource allocation.

Prioritizing Initiatives: Prioritize AI initiatives based on their potential impact, feasibility, and alignment with your business strategy.

3.4.3 Developing an Implementation Roadmap

Phased Approach: Develop a phased implementation roadmap that outlines key milestones and timelines. Starting with pilot projects or smaller initiatives can help in understanding the implications of AI integration and making necessary adjustments.

Resource Planning: Allocate resources, including budget, personnel, and technology, to support the implementation of your AI strategy.

3.4.4 Fostering an AI-Ready Culture

Employee Engagement: Engage your employees in the AI journey. Offer training and development opportunities to build AI literacy and skills within your team.

Promoting Collaboration: Encourage collaboration between different departments and teams to ensure a cohesive approach to AI integration.

3.4.5 Ensuring Ethical and Responsible AI Use

Developing Ethical Guidelines: Establish guidelines for ethical and responsible use of AI. This should cover aspects like data privacy, bias mitigation, and transparency.

Stakeholder Communication: Maintain open communication with stakeholders, including employees, customers, and partners, about your AI initiatives and their implications.

3.4.6 Monitoring, Learning, and Adapting

Performance Tracking: Regularly monitor the performance of your AI implementations against your set goals. Use these insights to refine and improve your AI strategy.

Adaptive Learning: Stay adaptable and be willing to learn and evolve your strategy based on new developments in AI technology and changing market conditions.

Conclusion

Building a comprehensive AI strategy for GPT-4 involves careful planning, clear goal setting, resource allocation, and the development of an AI-ready culture. By following these guidelines, businesses can effectively integrate AI into their operations, driving innovation and competitive advantage in the digital economy.

Chapter 4: Content Creation with GPT-4

In the digital age, content is king. This chapter delves into how GPT-4 is revolutionizing content creation, offering unparalleled efficiency and creativity. We will explore the diverse applications of GPT-4 in content generation and the strategies to leverage its capabilities effectively.

4.1 Understanding GPT-4's Capabilities in Content Creation

4.1.1 Language Proficiency: GPT-4's advanced natural language processing allows it to produce content that is not only grammatically correct but also contextually relevant and engaging.

4.1.2 Versatility Across Formats: Explore GPT-4's ability to create various types of content, from blog posts and articles to social media updates and creative writing.

4.2 Blogging and Article Writing with GPT-4

4.2.1 Enhancing Productivity: Learn how GPT-4 can be used to generate ideas, outlines, and even complete drafts for blogs and articles, significantly reducing the time and effort required.

4.2.2 Maintaining Quality and Originality: Strategies for ensuring that the content generated by GPT-4 remains unique, high-quality, and aligned with your brand voice.

4.3 Social Media and Engagement

4.3.1 Crafting Engaging Posts: Utilize GPT-4 to create compelling and original social media content that resonates with your audience.

4.3.2 Automation and Personalization: Discover how GPT-4 can automate content creation for social media while personalizing it for different segments of your audience.

4.4 AI in Video and Podcast Scriptwriting

4.4.1 Script Creation: Delve into GPT-4's role in scripting for videos and podcasts, offering a new dimension of efficiency and creativity in multimedia content creation.

4.4.2 Enhancing Storytelling: Learn how GPT-4 can contribute to storytelling, creating engaging narratives and dialogue for various media formats.

4.5 Improving SEO with GPT-4

4.5.1 Keyword Integration: Understand how to use GPT-4 to optimize content for SEO, integrating keywords seamlessly without compromising the quality of the content.

4.5.2 Content Strategy and Analytics: Using GPT-4 to analyze content trends and develop strategies that align with SEO best practices.

4.6 Ethical Considerations in AI-Generated Content

4.6.1 Addressing Plagiarism Concerns: Strategies for ensuring that content generated by GPT-4 is original and does not infringe on copyright laws.

4.6.2 Balancing AI and Human Input: The importance of human oversight in AI-generated content to maintain authenticity and ethical standards.

Conclusion

Content creation with GPT-4 opens up a realm of possibilities for businesses and content creators. By harnessing the power of GPT-4, you can elevate the quality, efficiency, and impact of your content. This chapter provides the groundwork for understanding and utilizing GPT-4 in various content creation endeavors, setting the stage for innovative and effective communication in the digital space.

Blogging and Article Writing with GPT-4

In the realm of digital content, blogging and article writing are essential for engagement, information dissemination, and SEO. GPT-4 is transforming this space by automating and enhancing the content creation process.

4.2.1 Streamlining the Writing Process

Topic Generation: GPT-4 can generate a wide range of topics based on current trends, niche subjects, or specific keywords, providing a constant stream of ideas for bloggers and content creators.

Drafting Content: GPT-4 can create initial drafts for articles and blog posts. These drafts can serve as a starting point, significantly speeding up the writing process.

Editing and Refinement: Beyond drafting, GPT-4 can assist in editing and refining content, suggesting improvements in grammar, style, and coherence.

4.2.2 Enhancing Creativity and Quality

Creative Angles: GPT-4 can suggest unique angles and perspectives for articles, helping content stand out in a crowded digital landscape.

Consistency in Style and Tone: GPT-4 can be fine-tuned to maintain a consistent style and tone that aligns with your brand or personal voice, ensuring a uniform reading experience.

4.2.3 Increasing Efficiency and Productivity

Speeding Up Content Production: By automating various stages of the writing process, GPT-4 enables content creators to produce quality articles in a fraction of the time.

Scalability: With GPT-4, scaling up content production becomes feasible, allowing for a more robust content strategy without compromising on quality.

4.2.4 SEO Optimization

Keyword Integration: GPT-4 can optimize content for SEO by naturally incorporating relevant keywords, enhancing the visibility of your articles in search engine results.

SEO-Friendly Formats: GPT-4 can structure articles in SEO-friendly formats, using appropriate headers, meta descriptions, and optimized content layouts.

4.2.5 Addressing Challenges and Limitations

Authenticity: While GPT-4 can generate content, human intervention is crucial to ensure the authenticity and genuineness of the articles.

Fact-Checking: Articles generated by GPT-4 should be fact-checked, as AI may inadvertently include inaccuracies or outdated information.

Plagiarism Concerns: Use plagiarism checkers to ensure the originality of AI-generated content, maintaining ethical writing standards.

4.2.6 Best Practices for Using GPT-4 in Content Creation

Collaborative Approach: Use GPT-4 as a collaborative tool, combining AI efficiency with human creativity and insight.

Customization and Fine-Tuning: Customize GPT-4's outputs according to your specific needs and audience, and fine-tune the AI for better alignment with your content goals.

Conclusion

GPT-4's capabilities in blogging and article writing represent a significant advancement in content creation. By leveraging this technology, content creators can enhance their productivity, creativity, and SEO effectiveness, all while maintaining high standards of quality and authenticity.

Social Media and Engagement with GPT-4

Social media is a dynamic and crucial platform for engagement, branding, and marketing. GPT-4 is redefining how businesses and individuals create and manage their social media presence.

4.3.1 Crafting Impactful Social Media Content

Generating Engaging Posts: Use GPT-4 to generate creative, engaging posts that capture the essence of your brand and resonate with your audience. GPT-4 can help in crafting catchy headlines, compelling narratives, and relevant hashtags.

Content Diversification: With GPT-4, diversify your content types – from text-based posts to ideas for infographics, polls, and interactive content. This variety can help in maintaining an engaging and vibrant social media presence.

4.3.2 Personalization and Audience Engagement

Audience Analysis: Leverage GPT-4 to analyze audience data and preferences, enabling you to tailor your content to the interests and needs of your followers.

Interactive Communication: Utilize GPT-4's conversational capabilities to automate and personalize responses to comments and messages, enhancing audience engagement and building stronger relationships.

4.3.3 Automation and Scheduling

Efficient Content Management: GPT-4 can assist in scheduling and automating posts, ensuring a consistent and timely social media presence. This automation can be a significant time-saver, especially for businesses with a broad social media footprint.

Campaign Management: Use GPT-4 for managing and optimizing social media campaigns. It can analyze campaign performance data, suggesting adjustments for improved engagement and reach.

4.3.4 Enhancing Brand Voice and Consistency

Brand Voice Alignment: GPT-4 can be trained to emulate your brand's unique voice and style, ensuring consistency across all social media posts and interactions.

Multilingual Content Creation: For global brands, GPT-4's multilingual capabilities allow for the creation of region-specific content, making your social media strategy more inclusive and effective.

4.3.5 Monitoring and Analytics

Sentiment Analysis: Employ GPT-4 to conduct sentiment analysis on social media interactions, gaining insights into public perception and feedback on your brand.

Performance Analytics: GPT-4 can assist in analyzing social media metrics, providing actionable insights for strategy refinement and content optimization.

4.3.6 Overcoming Challenges and Ethical Considerations

Maintaining Authenticity: While leveraging AI for content creation, it's crucial to maintain authenticity and human touch in your social media interactions.

Data Privacy and Ethics: Be mindful of privacy concerns and ethical considerations when using AI to analyze audience data and interactions.

Conclusion

Incorporating GPT-4 into social media strategy offers immense potential for enhancing engagement, personalization, and efficiency. By creatively using GPT-4 for content creation and analytics, businesses and individuals can elevate their social media presence, foster stronger audience relationships, and stay ahead in the ever-evolving digital landscape.

AI in Video and Podcast Production with GPT-4

The landscape of video and podcast production is rapidly evolving with the advent of AI technologies like GPT-4. This section explores how GPT-4 is transforming these mediums, offering new levels of efficiency and creativity.

4.4.1 Revolutionizing Scriptwriting and Storyboarding

Automated Scriptwriting: GPT-4 can assist in generating scripts for videos and podcasts, providing a base for creative storytelling. Its ability to understand context and narrative structure allows for the creation of coherent and engaging scripts.

Storyboarding and Conceptualization: GPT-4 can be used to conceptualize storyboards and outlines, helping creators visualize the flow and structure of their content before production begins.

4.4.2 Enhancing Creativity in Content Creation

Creative Input: GPT-4 can offer creative suggestions for dialogue, plot development, and character creation, adding depth and diversity to content.

Genre-Specific Content: GPT-4's versatility allows it to adapt to various genres, whether it's crafting humorous segments for a podcast or developing a suspenseful narrative for a video.

4.4.3 Personalizing Content for Target Audiences

Audience Analysis: Utilize GPT-4 to analyze audience preferences and trends, enabling the creation of content that resonates more effectively with your target audience.

Customization: GPT-4 can tailor content to different audience segments, enhancing personalization and relevance.

4.4.4 Streamlining Post-Production Processes

Automated Editing Assistance: GPT-4 can assist in the post-production process by suggesting edits, sequencing ideas, and even generating descriptive content for videos and podcasts.

Subtitle and Caption Generation: Use GPT-4 to efficiently generate accurate subtitles and captions, a crucial aspect of making content accessible to a wider audience.

4.4.5 Integrating AI in Marketing and Distribution

Promotional Content Creation: GPT-4 can be used to create promotional materials for your videos and podcasts, such as social media posts, email newsletters, or blog entries.

SEO Optimization: Leverage GPT-4 to optimize descriptions and tags for better search engine visibility and audience reach.

4.4.6 Addressing Challenges and Ethical Considerations

Preserving Authenticity: While AI can enhance the creative process, it's important to preserve the authentic voice and essence of the content, ensuring it resonates with human audiences.

Copyright and Originality Concerns: Be vigilant about copyright issues and ensure the originality of AI-generated content, especially in scriptwriting and storytelling.

Conclusion

GPT-4's application in video and podcast production opens up new avenues for creators, enabling them to push the boundaries of storytelling, efficiency, and audience engagement. By harnessing the capabilities of AI, content creators can not only streamline their production processes but also infuse a level of innovation and personalization that sets their content apart in a crowded digital space.

Chapter 5: AI-Driven Marketing and SEO

The integration of AI, particularly GPT-4, in marketing and SEO (Search Engine Optimization) is transforming how businesses approach digital marketing strategies. This chapter explores the various applications and benefits of using GPT-4 in marketing and SEO.

5.1 Revolutionizing Digital Marketing with GPT-4

5.1.1 Tailored Marketing Strategies: GPT-4's data processing capabilities enable businesses to analyze market trends and consumer behaviors, leading to more tailored and effective marketing strategies.

5.1.2 Enhanced Customer Insights: Use GPT-4 to gain deeper insights into customer preferences and patterns, allowing for more targeted and personalized marketing campaigns.

5.2 Search Engine Optimization and GPT-4

5.2.1 Optimizing Content for Search Engines: GPT-4 can assist in creating SEO-friendly content that not only ranks higher in search engine results but also engages readers.

5.2.2 Keyword Analysis and Integration: Leverage GPT-4's capabilities to identify and integrate relevant keywords into your content, enhancing its visibility and reach.

5.3 Personalizing Customer Experiences

5.3.1 Dynamic Content Personalization: GPT-4 enables the dynamic personalization of content, ensuring that each interaction with customers is relevant and engaging.

5.3.2 Predictive Consumer Behavior Modeling: Utilize GPT-4 to predict consumer behaviors and preferences, allowing for more proactive and personalized marketing approaches.

5.4 Automating and Optimizing Ad Campaigns

5.4.1 Efficient Campaign Management: GPT-4 can automate routine tasks in campaign management, such as ad placements and adjustments based on performance data.

5.4.2 Real-time Optimization: Implement GPT-4 to continuously analyze and optimize marketing campaigns in real-time, ensuring maximum efficiency and ROI.

5.5 Enhancing Content Creation for Marketing

5.5.1 Creative and Engaging Content: Use GPT-4 to generate creative marketing content, from email campaigns to social media posts, that resonates with your audience.

5.5.2 Multichannel Content Strategy: Employ GPT-4 to create a cohesive content strategy across various channels, maintaining a consistent brand voice and message.

5.6 Navigating the Challenges in AI-Driven Marketing

5.6.1 Balancing Automation and Human Touch: While leveraging AI in marketing, it's crucial to maintain the human element in your messaging and interactions.

5.6.2 Addressing Privacy and Ethical Concerns: Be mindful of privacy and ethical considerations in data usage and AI applications in marketing.

Conclusion

AI-driven marketing and SEO, powered by GPT-4, offer unparalleled advantages in terms of efficiency, personalization, and insight. This chapter provides a roadmap for harnessing these capabilities to enhance your digital marketing strategies, ensuring that your business stays competitive and relevant in the rapidly evolving digital landscape.

Search Engine Optimization with GPT-4

In the digital marketing world, SEO is vital for visibility and success. GPT-4 is revolutionizing SEO by providing tools to create more effective and optimized content. This section delves into how GPT-4 can be utilized to enhance SEO strategies.

5.2.1 Understanding GPT-4's Role in SEO

Content Quality and Relevance: GPT-4 can generate high-quality, relevant content that aligns with search engine algorithms, improving the chances of ranking higher in search results.

Semantic Search Capabilities: Leverage GPT-4's understanding of semantic search, where it comprehends user intent and context, to create content that better aligns with what users are searching for.

5.2.2 Keyword Research and Optimization

Advanced Keyword Analysis: Utilize GPT-4 to analyze large volumes of data and identify effective keywords and phrases that can drive traffic to your site.

Integrating Keywords Naturally: GPT-4's natural language processing ensures that keywords are integrated seamlessly into content, maintaining readability and engagement.

5.2.3 Creating SEO-Friendly Content

Structuring Content for SEO: GPT-4 can help structure articles, blog posts, and web content in a way that's optimized for search engines, including the use of headers, meta descriptions, and alt tags.

Rich and Varied Content Types: Encourage the use of GPT-4 to generate diverse content types, such as how-to guides, listicles, and long-form articles, all of which can contribute positively to SEO.

5.2.4 Enhancing User Experience

Readability and Engagement: Use GPT-4 to improve the readability and engagement of your content, which are key factors in SEO ranking.

Personalized Content: GPT-4 can aid in creating personalized content for different segments of your audience, improving user experience and engagement.

5.2.5 Keeping Up with SEO Trends

Adapting to Algorithm Changes: Stay ahead of SEO trends and algorithm changes with GPT-4's ability to quickly analyze and adapt to new patterns and requirements.

Continuous Learning and Updating: GPT-4's learning capabilities mean it can continuously update its understanding of SEO best practices, keeping your strategies effective.

5.2.6 Addressing Challenges and Limitations

Avoiding Over-Reliance on Automation: While GPT-4 is a powerful tool for SEO, it's important to combine its capabilities with human oversight to ensure content authenticity and compliance with SEO guidelines.

Monitoring and Adjusting Strategies: Regularly review and adjust your SEO strategies, as relying solely on AI-generated insights may not always capture the nuances of human search behaviors.

Conclusion

GPT-4 offers significant advantages in optimizing websites and content for search engines. By leveraging its capabilities in keyword research, content creation, and trend analysis, you can significantly enhance your SEO efforts, driving more traffic and engagement to your site.

Personalizing Customer Experiences with GPT-4

Personalization is a key differentiator in today's competitive market. GPT-4 is enabling businesses to personalize customer experiences at scale, enhancing satisfaction and loyalty. This section explores how GPT-4 can be applied to create highly personalized interactions and experiences.

5.3.1 Understanding the Customer

Data-Driven Insights: Utilize GPT-4 to analyze customer data, such as browsing history, purchase patterns, and preferences, to gain a deeper understanding of each customer.

Segmentation and Profiling: Leverage GPT-4's capabilities to segment customers into distinct profiles, allowing for more targeted and relevant interactions.

5.3.2 Tailoring Content and Recommendations

Personalized Content Creation: Use GPT-4 to generate personalized content, such as emails, product descriptions, and website copy, that resonates with individual customers' interests and needs.

Dynamic Product Recommendations: Implement GPT-4 to provide dynamic product recommendations based on customer behaviors, increasing the relevance and effectiveness of your offerings.

5.3.3 Enhancing Customer Service

Automated Personalized Responses: Employ GPT-4 in customer service to provide quick, personalized responses to inquiries, improving customer satisfaction and engagement.

Understanding and Anticipating Needs: GPT-4 can help anticipate customer needs based on past interactions, offering proactive service and support.

5.3.4 Creating Engaging Customer Journeys

Personalized Marketing Campaigns: Develop personalized marketing campaigns using GPT-4's insights, ensuring that each customer receives relevant and engaging messages.

Customized User Experiences: Tailor the user experience on websites and apps using GPT-4, from personalized greetings to content that aligns with the user's preferences.

5.3.5 Measuring and Optimizing Customer Interactions

Feedback Analysis: Analyze customer feedback and reviews using GPT-4 to understand sentiments and improve offerings.

Continuous Improvement: Continuously refine personalization strategies based on GPT-4's analysis and customer interaction data.

5.3.6 Addressing Privacy and Ethical Concerns

Respecting Customer Privacy: Ensure that personalization efforts with GPT-4 adhere to privacy laws and ethical guidelines, maintaining transparency and customer trust.

Balancing Personalization and Intrusiveness: Find the right balance between personalization and intrusiveness, ensuring that efforts to tailor experiences do not compromise customer comfort or privacy.

Conclusion

The use of GPT-4 in personalizing customer experiences offers a powerful way to enhance customer engagement and loyalty. By leveraging AI to understand and anticipate customer needs, businesses can create more meaningful, relevant, and satisfying experiences for their customers.

Automating and Optimizing Ad Campaigns with GPT-4

In today's digital marketplace, the efficiency and effectiveness of advertising campaigns are crucial for business success. GPT-4 is transforming ad campaigns by automating and optimizing various aspects of advertising. This section explores the role of GPT-4 in enhancing digital advertising strategies.

5.4.1 Streamlining Campaign Management

Automated Ad Creation: Utilize GPT-4's capabilities to automatically generate compelling ad copy and creative content, tailored to different platforms and audiences.

Campaign Setup and Management: Employ GPT-4 to streamline the setup and ongoing management of ad campaigns, reducing manual effort and increasing efficiency.

5.4.2 Targeting and Personalization

Precise Audience Targeting: Leverage GPT-4's data analysis capabilities to identify and target specific audience segments, ensuring that your ads reach the most relevant viewers.

Dynamic Personalization: Use GPT-4 to personalize ads in real-time, based on user behavior and preferences, for higher engagement and conversion rates.

5.4.3 Performance Analysis and Optimization

Real-time Analytics: Implement GPT-4 to monitor and analyze campaign performance in real-time, providing insights into what is working and what isn't.

Optimization Algorithms: Utilize GPT-4's machine learning algorithms to continuously optimize ad campaigns, adjusting variables like bidding, placement, and content for optimal performance.

5.4.4 Enhancing Creative Testing

A/B Testing Automation: GPT-4 can automate the process of A/B testing different ad creatives and formats, quickly identifying the most effective options.

Creative Insights: Use GPT-4 to gain insights into creative elements that resonate with your audience, helping to inform future creative strategies.

5.4.5 Budget Management and ROI Improvement

Efficient Budget Allocation: Employ GPT-4 to manage ad budgets more efficiently, ensuring funds are allocated to the most effective campaigns and channels.

Maximizing ROI: GPT-4's ability to analyze large datasets helps in making informed decisions that maximize the return on investment for your ad spend.

5.4.6 Addressing Challenges in AI-Driven Advertising

Ethical Advertising Practices: Ensure that the use of GPT-4 in advertising adheres to ethical standards, avoiding manipulative or intrusive tactics.

Human Oversight: Maintain human oversight in AI-driven campaigns to ensure that ads remain relevant, appropriate, and effective, particularly in sensitive or complex market contexts.

Conclusion

GPT-4's role in automating and optimizing ad campaigns represents a significant advancement in digital advertising. By harnessing AI for targeting, personalization, analysis, and optimization, businesses can significantly enhance the effectiveness of their advertising efforts, driving better results and higher ROI.

Chapter 6: E-commerce and GPT-4

The integration of GPT-4 into e-commerce is reshaping the retail landscape, offering unprecedented opportunities for personalization, efficiency, and innovation. This chapter explores the multifaceted impact of GPT-4 on e-commerce operations.

6.1 Transforming Online Shopping Experience

6.1.1 Personalized Customer Interaction: GPT-4 can enhance the online shopping experience by providing personalized product recommendations and tailored content based on individual customer preferences and shopping history.

6.1.2 Enhanced Customer Service: Utilize GPT-4 powered chatbots for providing instant, accurate, and personalized customer service, from addressing queries to resolving issues.

6.2 Streamlining E-commerce Operations

6.2.1 Inventory Management: GPT-4 can help in predicting inventory needs, analyzing sales data, and automating restocking processes, thereby optimizing inventory management.

6.2.2 Order Processing and Fulfillment: Implement GPT-4 to streamline order processing and fulfillment operations, enhancing efficiency and reducing errors.

6.3 Improving Product Descriptions and Content

6.3.1 Automated Content Creation: GPT-4 can automatically generate compelling and SEO-friendly product descriptions, improving product visibility and attractiveness.

6.3.2 Dynamic Content Updates: Use GPT-4 to dynamically update content based on inventory changes, customer feedback, or market trends, keeping product listings fresh and relevant.

6.4 Enhancing Marketing and Sales Strategies

6.4.1 Targeted Marketing Campaigns: Leverage GPT-4's data analysis capabilities for developing targeted marketing campaigns, improving customer engagement and conversion rates.

6.4.2 Sales Forecasting: Employ GPT-4 for accurate sales forecasting, aiding in strategic decision-making and promotional planning.

6.5 Data Analysis and Business Insights

6.5.1 Consumer Behavior Analysis: Utilize GPT-4 to analyze consumer behavior, providing insights into purchasing patterns, preferences, and trends.

6.5.2 Market Trend Analysis: GPT-4 can assist in analyzing market trends and consumer sentiment, helping businesses stay ahead of the curve.

6.6 Navigating Challenges in E-commerce

6.6.1 Balancing Automation and Human Touch: While automation through GPT-4 enhances efficiency, maintaining a human touch in customer interactions is crucial for building trust and loyalty.

6.6.2 Ensuring Data Privacy and Security: In the use of AI for e-commerce, prioritize customer data privacy and security, adhering to regulations and ethical standards.

Conclusion

The application of GPT-4 in e-commerce presents a transformative opportunity for businesses to enhance their operations, customer experience, and strategic decision-making. By leveraging the capabilities of GPT-4, e-commerce platforms can achieve greater efficiency, personalization, and market responsiveness, driving growth and success in the digital retail space.

Enhancing Online Stores with AI

In the era of digital retail, AI, particularly GPT-4, is a game-changer for online stores. This section delves into how GPT-4 can be used to enhance various facets of e-commerce, driving sales and improving customer experiences.

6.2.1 Revolutionizing Customer Experience

Personalized Shopping Experiences: Implement GPT-4 to provide customers with personalized shopping experiences. AI can analyze past behaviors and preferences to recommend products, customize search results, and even tailor the website layout to individual users.

Interactive Product Discovery: Use GPT-4 to create interactive and engaging ways for customers to discover products, such as AI-driven quizzes, virtual try-ons, or personalized product tours.

6.2.2 Optimizing Website Content and Layout

Dynamic Content Creation: GPT-4 can assist in generating dynamic content for product descriptions, blogs, and marketing materials, ensuring that the content is always fresh, relevant, and SEO-friendly.

Website Layout Optimization: Leverage GPT-4's data analysis capabilities to optimize the layout of your online store, arranging products and categories based on customer preferences and shopping patterns.

6.2.3 Streamlining Operations and Logistics

Efficient Inventory Management: Employ GPT-4 for smart inventory management, predicting stock levels, and automating reordering processes, reducing overstock and stockouts.

Automated Order Processing: GPT-4 can help streamline order processing, from automated order confirmation to coordinating logistics, ensuring a smooth and efficient fulfillment process.

6.2.4 Enhancing Customer Service and Support

AI-Powered Customer Support: Integrate GPT-4 powered chatbots and virtual assistants to provide instant, 24/7 customer support, addressing queries, providing information, and resolving issues.

Feedback and Review Analysis: Utilize GPT-4 to analyze customer feedback and reviews, gaining insights to improve products and services continually.

6.2.5 Driving Marketing and Sales

Targeted Marketing Campaigns: Use GPT-4 to analyze customer data and create targeted, personalized marketing campaigns, increasing engagement and conversion rates.

Sales Prediction and Analysis: Leverage GPT-4's predictive capabilities to forecast sales trends, helping in planning and decision-making for promotions, stock, and marketing strategies.

6.2.6 Addressing the Challenges

Balancing Automation with Human Interaction: While AI can significantly enhance efficiency, maintaining a balance with human interaction is crucial to address complex customer needs and build relationships.

Data Privacy and Ethical Concerns: Ensure that the use of AI in your online store adheres to data privacy laws and ethical standards, maintaining customer trust and compliance.

Conclusion

Integrating GPT-4 into online stores opens up a world of possibilities for enhancing the customer experience, streamlining operations, and driving sales. By leveraging the power of AI, e-commerce businesses can not only meet the evolving expectations of digital consumers but also stay competitive in the rapidly changing retail landscape.

Predictive Analytics and Customer Insights with GPT-4

In the realm of e-commerce, understanding and anticipating customer needs is pivotal. GPT-4 empowers online businesses with predictive analytics and deep customer insights, driving informed decision-making and strategic planning.

6.3.1 Leveraging Predictive Analytics for Business Strategy

Anticipating Customer Needs: Utilize GPT-4 to analyze customer data and predict future buying patterns, preferences, and behaviors. This predictive insight allows businesses to proactively meet customer needs.

Inventory and Supply Chain Optimization: GPT-4 can forecast demand for products, helping in optimizing inventory levels and supply chain operations, thus reducing waste and improving efficiency.

6.3.2 Gaining Deeper Customer Insights

Understanding Customer Journeys: Use GPT-4 to map out detailed customer journeys, identifying key touchpoints and opportunities for engagement and conversion.

Segmentation and Targeting: GPT-4's ability to process vast datasets enables precise customer segmentation, allowing for targeted marketing efforts and personalized customer experiences.

6.3.3 Enhancing Product Development and Offerings

Product Development Insights: Analyze customer feedback and market trends using GPT-4 to inform product development, ensuring that new products align with customer needs and market demands.

Service Improvement: Employ GPT-4 to identify areas for service improvement by analyzing customer interactions and feedback, continually enhancing the customer experience.

6.3.4 Driving Marketing Effectiveness

Campaign Optimization: Leverage predictive analytics to optimize marketing campaigns, predicting which strategies will be most effective for different customer segments.

Content Personalization: Use GPT-4 to personalize marketing content based on predicted customer preferences, enhancing engagement and relevance.

6.3.5 Enhancing Customer Retention and Loyalty

Predicting Customer Churn: GPT-4 can identify patterns that indicate a risk of customer churn, enabling businesses to proactively engage and retain at-risk customers.

Loyalty Program Optimization: Utilize GPT-4 to tailor loyalty programs to individual customer preferences, enhancing satisfaction and loyalty.

6.3.6 Addressing Ethical Considerations

Data Privacy and Consent: Ensure that predictive analytics and customer data usage comply with data privacy laws and standards, maintaining transparency and customer trust.

Ethical Use of Predictive Insights: Be mindful of ethical considerations in using predictive insights, avoiding manipulation and respecting customer autonomy.

Conclusion

The application of GPT-4 in predictive analytics and customer insights offers e-commerce businesses a powerful tool for understanding and anticipating customer needs. By harnessing these insights, businesses can make data-driven decisions, tailor their offerings, and create more meaningful customer experiences, ultimately driving growth and customer loyalty.

Chatbots and Customer Service with GPT-4

In the digital era, chatbots powered by AI like GPT-4 are revolutionizing customer service. They offer instantaneous, efficient, and personalized customer interactions. This section examines how GPT-4 enhances customer service in e-commerce through advanced chatbots.

6.4.1 Transforming Customer Interactions

Instant Customer Support: GPT-4-powered chatbots can provide instant responses to customer inquiries, reducing wait times and improving overall customer satisfaction.

24/7 Availability: Unlike human agents, GPT-4 chatbots are available around the clock, offering consistent support regardless of time zones or holidays.

6.4.2 Personalized Customer Assistance

Tailored Responses: GPT-4 chatbots can deliver personalized assistance by analyzing customer data and previous interactions. This personalization makes each interaction more relevant and effective.

Product Recommendations: These chatbots can suggest products or services tailored to individual customer preferences, enhancing the shopping experience.

6.4.3 Handling Complex Queries

Understanding Complex Inquiries: GPT-4's advanced language understanding allows it to handle more complex customer queries than traditional chatbots, providing accurate and helpful responses.

Escalation to Human Agents: When necessary, GPT-4 chatbots can intelligently identify when to escalate complex issues to human customer service agents.

6.4.4 Enhancing Efficiency and Reducing Costs

Reduced Workload on Human Staff: By handling routine inquiries, GPT-4 chatbots can significantly reduce the workload on human customer service staff, allowing them to focus on more complex and high-value tasks.

Cost-Effective: Automating customer service with GPT-4 chatbots is a cost-effective solution, especially for businesses that face a high volume of customer interactions.

6.4.5 Continuous Learning and Improvement

Adaptive Learning: GPT-4 chatbots can learn from each interaction, continuously improving their responses and effectiveness over time.

Feedback Integration: Incorporate customer feedback into the chatbot's learning process, ensuring that it evolves in line with customer needs and preferences.

6.4.6 Overcoming Challenges and Building Trust

Transparency and Trust: Be transparent with customers about the use of AI in customer service. Building trust involves ensuring that chatbot interactions are respectful, helpful, and privacy-conscious.

Balancing AI and Human Elements: Maintain a balance between automated and human elements in customer service to ensure that customers feel valued and understood.

Conclusion

GPT-4-powered chatbots represent a significant leap forward in customer service for e-commerce. By providing personalized, efficient, and intelligent customer interactions, these AI-driven chatbots can enhance customer experience, streamline operations, and contribute to business growth and customer loyalty.

Chapter 7: Data Analysis and Business Intelligence with GPT-4

In today's data-driven world, leveraging AI for data analysis and business intelligence is crucial for informed decision-making and strategic planning. This chapter explores how GPT-4 can be used to transform data analysis and enhance business intelligence in various industries.

7.1 The Power of GPT-4 in Data Analysis

7.1.1 Advanced Data Processing: GPT-4 can process and analyze vast amounts of data far beyond human capacity, uncovering patterns, trends, and insights that might otherwise go unnoticed.

7.1.2 Real-time Analysis: Utilize GPT-4 for real-time data analysis, providing businesses with the ability to make quick, informed decisions based on the latest information.

7.2 Enhancing Business Intelligence

7.2.1 Predictive Analytics: Employ GPT-4 in predictive analytics to forecast future market trends, customer behaviors, and business outcomes, aiding in proactive decision-making.

7.2.2 Competitive Intelligence: Use GPT-4 to gather and analyze data on competitors, providing insights into market positioning, strategy, and potential opportunities.

7.3 Optimizing Operational Efficiency

7.3.1 Streamlining Business Processes: Implement GPT-4 to identify inefficiencies in business processes, recommending optimizations that can save time and reduce costs.

7.3.2 Automation of Routine Tasks: Leverage GPT-4 to automate routine data analysis tasks, freeing up human resources for more complex and strategic activities.

7.4 Driving Innovation and Growth

7.4.1 Identifying New Opportunities: GPT-4 can help businesses identify new market opportunities, emerging trends, and areas for innovation, driving growth and expansion.

7.4.2 Enhancing Product Development: Utilize GPT-4's insights to inform product development, ensuring that new offerings align with customer needs and market demand.

7.5 Improving Customer Insights and Personalization

7.5.1 Deep Customer Understanding: Use GPT-4 to gain a deeper understanding of customer preferences, behaviors, and needs, enhancing the ability to personalize products and services.

7.5.2 Targeted Marketing Strategies: Leverage GPT-4's analysis to develop more targeted and effective marketing strategies, increasing engagement and conversion rates.

7.6 Addressing Challenges in AI-Driven Analytics

7.6.1 Ensuring Data Accuracy and Quality: Maintain a focus on the quality and accuracy of data used in GPT-4 analysis to ensure reliable insights.

7.6.2 Ethical Considerations and Privacy: Be mindful of ethical considerations and privacy concerns in the use of AI for data analysis, ensuring compliance with regulations and ethical standards.

Conclusion

GPT-4's role in data analysis and business intelligence is transformative, offering businesses the ability to harness the power of their data for strategic advantage. By integrating GPT-4 into data-driven processes, businesses can unlock new levels of insight, efficiency, and innovation, paving the way for informed decision-making and sustained growth.

Harnessing Data for Strategic Decisions with GPT-4

In an increasingly data-centric business world, the ability to harness data effectively for strategic decision-making is critical. GPT-4, with its advanced analytics capabilities, plays a pivotal role in transforming raw data into actionable insights.

7.1.1 Data-Driven Strategy Development

Comprehensive Data Analysis: GPT-4 can analyze a wide array of data sources, from market trends to customer feedback, providing a comprehensive overview for strategic planning.

Identifying Key Metrics: Use GPT-4 to identify and monitor key performance indicators (KPIs) that are crucial for your business strategy, ensuring data-driven decisions.

7.1.2 Uncovering Market and Consumer Insights

Market Trend Analysis: Employ GPT-4 to stay ahead of market trends, analyzing current and historical data to predict future market developments.

Consumer Behavior Insights: Leverage GPT-4 to gain a deeper understanding of consumer behaviors and preferences, tailoring strategies to meet customer needs effectively.

7.1.3 Risk Assessment and Management

Predictive Risk Analysis: Utilize GPT-4's predictive capabilities to assess potential risks in business strategies, allowing for proactive risk management.

Scenario Planning: Use GPT-4 to simulate different business scenarios, evaluating the potential outcomes and risks associated with each.

7.1.4 Enhancing Operational Decision-Making

Operational Efficiency: Apply GPT-4's insights to optimize operational processes, from supply chain management to resource allocation, enhancing efficiency and reducing costs.

Productivity Improvement: GPT-4 can identify bottlenecks and areas for improvement in operational workflows, contributing to overall productivity enhancement.

7.1.5 Strategic Financial Planning

Financial Forecasting: Leverage GPT-4 for accurate financial forecasting, aiding in budgeting, financial planning, and investment decisions.

Resource Allocation: Utilize GPT-4's insights for effective resource allocation, ensuring that investments and resources are directed towards areas with the highest potential for return.

7.1.6 Navigating Ethical and Compliance Issues

Data Privacy and Compliance: Ensure that the use of GPT-4 in data analysis complies with data privacy laws and regulations.

Ethical Decision-Making: Be mindful of ethical considerations in strategic decision-making, using data insights responsibly and transparently.

Conclusion

Harnessing the power of data for strategic decision-making with GPT-4 offers businesses a competitive edge. By translating complex data into actionable insights, GPT-4 empowers businesses to make informed, strategic decisions that drive growth, efficiency, and innovation.

Predictive Modelling and Trend Analysis with GPT-4

Predictive modelling and trend analysis are essential in anticipating future market movements and consumer behaviors. GPT-4's advanced AI capabilities make it an invaluable tool in these analytical processes, providing businesses with foresight and strategic advantage.

7.2.1 Leveraging Predictive Modelling

Forecasting Market Trends: Employ GPT-4 to analyze historical data and current market signals to forecast future trends, enabling businesses to stay ahead in their market planning.

Predicting Consumer Behavior: Utilize GPT-4 to model and predict consumer behavior patterns, helping in tailoring marketing and sales strategies to future customer needs and preferences.

7.2.2 Enhancing Trend Analysis

Identifying Emerging Trends: Use GPT-4 to sift through vast datasets and social media content to identify emerging trends, giving businesses the early mover advantage in new markets and product developments.

Sector-Specific Trend Analysis: Leverage GPT-4 for in-depth trend analysis in specific sectors, providing insights that are tailored to industry-specific challenges and opportunities.

7.2.3 Data-Driven Decision Making

Strategic Business Decisions: GPT-4's predictive models can inform strategic business decisions, from product development to market entry strategies, ensuring they are data-driven and forward-looking.

Risk Assessment and Mitigation: Employ GPT-4's predictive analysis to assess potential risks in business decisions, enabling proactive mitigation strategies.

7.2.4 Optimizing Operations and Supply Chain

Operational Forecasting: Use GPT-4 to predict operational needs, from staffing to inventory management, optimizing efficiency and reducing operational costs.

Supply Chain Optimization: GPT-4 can assist in anticipating supply chain disruptions and demand fluctuations, enabling more resilient and responsive supply chain strategies.

7.2.5 Customizing Customer Experiences

Personalized Marketing and Sales: Utilize trend analysis and predictive modelling to create personalized marketing and sales campaigns, enhancing customer engagement and conversion rates.

Product Recommendation Systems: Implement GPT-4 to develop sophisticated product recommendation systems, enhancing the customer shopping experience through personalized suggestions.

7.2.6 Addressing Challenges and Ethical Considerations

Accuracy and Reliability: Ensure the accuracy and reliability of predictive models and trend analysis, continuously validating and refining models based on new data.

Ethical Use of Predictive Insights: Be vigilant about the ethical use of predictive insights, avoiding biases in models and respecting customer privacy and data security.

Conclusion

Predictive modelling and trend analysis with GPT-4 are transforming how businesses anticipate and respond to future challenges and opportunities. By harnessing these AI capabilities, businesses can gain valuable foresight, enabling them to make strategic decisions that are informed, proactive, and tailored to emerging market and consumer trends.

Competitive Intelligence with AI

In today's fast-paced business environment, staying ahead of the competition is crucial. AI, particularly GPT-4, offers powerful tools for gaining competitive intelligence, providing businesses with critical insights to stay ahead in the market.

7.3.1 Harnessing AI for Market Analysis

In-depth Market Understanding: Employ GPT-4 to analyze vast amounts of market data, providing a comprehensive understanding of current market dynamics, trends, and potential shifts.

Identifying Market Opportunities: Leverage GPT-4's analytical capabilities to identify untapped market opportunities and areas where competitors may be overlooking.

7.3.2 Monitoring Competitor Activities

Real-time Competitor Tracking: Use GPT-4 to monitor competitor activities in real-time, from new product launches to marketing strategies and customer feedback.

Analyzing Competitor Strategies: GPT-4 can help dissect and understand competitor strategies, providing insights into their strengths and weaknesses.

7.3.3 Enhancing Strategic Planning

Strategic Decision-Making: Utilize competitive intelligence gathered by GPT-4 to inform strategic planning and decision-making, ensuring that strategies are responsive to the competitive landscape.

Scenario Planning: Leverage AI to simulate various competitive scenarios, helping businesses prepare for different market developments.

7.3.4 Improving Product and Service Offerings

Product Development Insights: Use AI-driven insights to refine and develop products and services that better meet market needs and differentiate from competitors.

Service Innovation: GPT-4 can identify gaps in competitors' service offerings, suggesting areas where your business can innovate and excel.

7.3.5 Targeting and Positioning

Effective Market Positioning: Employ GPT-4's insights for effective market positioning, identifying niches or segments where your business can achieve a competitive advantage.

Targeted Marketing Strategies: Utilize AI to develop targeted marketing strategies that effectively counteract competitors' moves and resonate with your audience.

7.3.6 Navigating Ethical Considerations

Ethical Data Usage: Ensure that the use of AI for competitive intelligence adheres to ethical standards and legal regulations, particularly regarding data sourcing and usage.

Responsible Intelligence Gathering: Maintain a responsible approach to intelligence gathering, focusing on openly available data and avoiding any deceptive or intrusive methods.

Conclusion

Competitive intelligence with AI, especially GPT-4, equips businesses with a profound understanding of their competitive environment. By harnessing the power of AI for competitive analysis, businesses can gain strategic insights, make informed decisions, and maintain a competitive edge in their respective markets.

Chapter 8: Ethical Considerations and Best Practices in AI

As AI technologies like GPT-4 become more integral to business and daily life, ethical considerations and best practices are paramount. This chapter delves into the ethical landscape of AI usage, focusing on how to responsibly integrate GPT-4 into various applications while adhering to high ethical standards.

8.1 Understanding AI Ethics

8.1.1 The Importance of Ethical AI: Discuss the significance of ethical considerations in AI development and deployment, emphasizing the impact on society, economy, and individual rights.

8.1.2 Key Ethical Principles in AI: Explore the key principles of ethical AI, including fairness, transparency, accountability, and privacy.

8.2 Data Privacy and Security

8.2.1 Protecting User Data: Examine strategies for protecting user data in AI applications, aligning with data protection laws like GDPR and CCPA.

8.2.2 Ensuring Data Security: Discuss the importance of implementing robust data security measures to prevent breaches and unauthorized access to sensitive information.

8.3 Addressing Bias and Fairness

8.3.1 Identifying and Mitigating Bias: Tackle the issue of bias in AI algorithms, including how to identify and mitigate biases in data sets and model development.

8.3.2 Promoting Fairness: Emphasize the importance of developing AI systems that are fair and do not discriminate against any group of users.

8.4 Transparency and Explainability

8.4.1 The Need for Transparency: Discuss why transparency in AI algorithms and decision-making processes is crucial for trust and accountability.

8.4.2 Advancing Explainability: Delve into the challenges and approaches to making AI decisions understandable to users and stakeholders.

8.5 Responsible AI Deployment

8.5.1 Best Practices in AI Deployment: Outline best practices for the responsible deployment of AI technologies, including GPT-4, in various sectors.

8.5.2 Continuous Monitoring and Evaluation: Advocate for the continuous monitoring and evaluation of AI systems to ensure they operate as intended and adhere to ethical standards.

8.6 AI and Societal Impact

8.6.1 Understanding Societal Implications: Explore the broader societal implications of AI, including potential impacts on employment, equity, and social norms.

8.6.2 Engaging with Stakeholders: Highlight the importance of engaging with a broad range of stakeholders, including policymakers, consumers, and advocacy groups, to guide responsible AI development.

8.7 Fostering an Ethical AI Culture

8.7.1 Building Ethical Awareness: Discuss strategies for building awareness and understanding of AI ethics within organizations.

8.7.2 Training and Education: Emphasize the role of training and education in fostering an ethical AI culture among developers, users, and decision-makers.

Conclusion

The ethical deployment and use of AI technologies like GPT-4 are critical in ensuring that these advancements benefit society as a whole. This chapter underscores the importance of ethical considerations and best practices in AI, advocating for responsible, fair, and transparent AI systems that respect user privacy and promote societal well-being.

Navigating Legal and Ethical Boundaries in AI

As AI technologies like GPT-4 become more prevalent, it's crucial to navigate the legal and ethical boundaries they present. This section provides insights into the challenges and strategies for legally and ethically implementing AI in various sectors.

8.2 Navigating Legal Boundaries

8.2.1 Understanding AI Regulations: Delve into current regulations governing AI, such as data protection laws (GDPR, CCPA), and discuss their implications for AI deployment and usage.

8.2.2 Compliance Strategies: Outline strategies for ensuring compliance with these regulations, emphasizing the importance of staying informed about evolving legal landscapes.

8.3 Ethical Considerations in AI Deployment

8.3.1 Addressing Ethical Challenges: Explore the ethical challenges posed by AI, including potential biases, decision-making transparency, and impacts on workforce dynamics.

8.3.2 Developing Ethical Guidelines: Discuss the development of ethical guidelines for AI usage, emphasizing fairness, accountability, and harm prevention.

8.4 Balancing Innovation and Responsibility

8.4.1 Responsible Innovation: Advocate for a balance between innovation and responsibility, ensuring that AI development considers ethical implications and societal impact.

8.4.2 Engaging with Ethical Dilemmas: Encourage a proactive approach to ethical dilemmas in AI, involving diverse perspectives and multidisciplinary approaches.

8.5 Privacy and Data Security

8.5.1 Prioritizing Data Privacy: Emphasize the importance of data privacy in AI applications, particularly in sectors handling sensitive information.

8.5.2 Implementing Data Security Measures: Provide guidance on implementing robust data security measures to protect against breaches and unauthorized access.

8.6 Addressing AI Bias and Discrimination

8.6.1 Identifying Sources of Bias: Explore how biases can enter AI systems and the importance of identifying and mitigating these biases.

8.6.2 Promoting Diversity and Inclusion: Highlight the role of diversity and inclusion in AI development teams as a strategy to reduce bias and promote fairness.

8.7 Transparency and Accountability

8.7.1 Ensuring Transparency: Discuss the need for transparency in AI algorithms and decision-making processes, fostering trust and understanding among users.

8.7.2 Building Accountability Mechanisms: Advocate for the establishment of accountability mechanisms in AI systems, ensuring responsible usage and recourse in case of errors or misuse.

Conclusion

Navigating the legal and ethical boundaries of AI is a complex but essential task. It requires a comprehensive understanding of regulations, ethical principles, privacy concerns, and the potential biases inherent in AI systems. By addressing these challenges proactively and responsibly, businesses and individuals can harness the power of AI technologies like GPT-4 in a manner that is beneficial, ethical, and compliant with legal standards.

Ensuring Privacy and Data Security in AI Applications

In the era of AI and big data, ensuring the privacy and security of data is paramount. This section addresses the critical importance of safeguarding user information in AI applications, especially when utilizing advanced technologies like GPT-4.

8.5.1 Importance of Data Privacy and Security

Understanding the Stakes: Highlight the significance of data privacy and security in AI, stressing the potential consequences of data breaches and misuse, including loss of public trust and legal repercussions.

Legal Compliance: Discuss the necessity of complying with international data protection regulations, such as GDPR in Europe and various state-level laws in the United States like the CCPA.

8.5.2 Implementing Robust Data Protection Measures

Secure Data Handling: Outline best practices for secure data handling, including secure storage, encryption, and controlled access to sensitive data.

Data Minimization and Anonymization: Advocate for data minimization and anonymization practices, ensuring that only necessary data is collected and processed, and personal identifiers are removed when possible.

8.5.3 Building Transparent Data Policies

Transparent Data Usage: Emphasize the importance of transparent data policies that clearly communicate to users how their data is being used and for what purposes.

User Consent and Control: Discuss the need for explicit user consent for data collection and processing, offering users control over their data, including the ability to opt-out and request data deletion.

8.5.4 Regular Audits and Compliance Checks

Conducting Regular Audits: Stress the importance of conducting regular audits to ensure ongoing compliance with data protection laws and internal data security policies.

Staying Updated with Regulations: Highlight the need to stay informed about changes in data protection laws and update practices accordingly.

8.5.5 Addressing AI-Specific Challenges

AI and Privacy: Delve into the specific challenges AI poses to privacy, such as the potential for uncovering hidden patterns in data that may inadvertently expose personal information.

Secure AI Development: Discuss secure AI development practices to prevent vulnerabilities in AI systems that could be exploited for data breaches.

8.5.6 Fostering a Culture of Data Security

Educating Employees: Advocate for regular employee training on data protection best practices and the importance of data security.

Building a Security-Minded Culture: Encourage the development of a security-minded culture within organizations, where data protection is a shared responsibility.

Conclusion

In the context of AI and particularly GPT-4, ensuring privacy and data security is not just a legal requirement but a fundamental aspect of ethical practice. By implementing robust data protection measures, maintaining transparency, and fostering a culture of security, businesses can protect user data, build trust, and harness the power of AI responsibly.

Responsible Use of AI Technologies

As AI technologies like GPT-4 become increasingly integral in various sectors, responsible usage becomes crucial. This section outlines the key aspects of responsible AI use, ensuring that AI technologies are employed in ways that are beneficial, ethical, and sustainable.

8.6.1 Understanding the Impact of AI

Comprehending AI's Reach: Discuss the widespread impact of AI on society, business, and individuals, emphasizing the need to understand AI's potential and limitations.

Assessing Impact on Workforce: Delve into AI's impact on the workforce, discussing the balance between automation and human employment, and the importance of reskilling initiatives.

8.6.2 Ethical AI Development and Deployment

Incorporating Ethical Considerations: Highlight the importance of incorporating ethical considerations into AI development and deployment, ensuring that AI acts in the best interests of society.

Avoiding Harmful Bias: Discuss strategies to avoid and mitigate biases in AI algorithms, promoting fairness and avoiding discrimination.

8.6.3 Ensuring Transparency and Accountability

Maintaining Transparency: Advocate for transparency in AI algorithms and decision-making processes, allowing users and stakeholders to understand how AI decisions are made.

Building Accountability Frameworks: Emphasize the need for accountability in AI systems, ensuring that there are mechanisms to address any issues or harms caused by AI decisions.

8.6.4 Promoting Privacy and Data Security

Prioritizing User Privacy: Stress the importance of prioritizing user privacy in AI applications, respecting user consent and data protection laws.

Safeguarding Data Security: Discuss the need for robust data security measures in AI systems to protect sensitive information from breaches and unauthorized access.

8.6.5 Sustainable and Inclusive AI Practices

Fostering Inclusivity: Highlight the importance of developing AI technologies that are inclusive and accessible to diverse populations.

Supporting Sustainable Practices: Advocate for the use of AI in supporting sustainable practices, contributing to environmental conservation and responsible resource usage.

8.6.6 Continuous Learning and Adaptation

Emphasizing Continuous Improvement: Encourage a culture of continuous learning and adaptation in AI usage, ensuring that AI systems evolve in response to new information, feedback, and societal changes.

Engaging in Ongoing Dialogue: Promote ongoing dialogue among technologists, policymakers, and other stakeholders to address emerging challenges and opportunities in AI.

Conclusion

Responsible use of AI technologies is not just a compliance issue; it's a commitment to ethical practices, societal well-being, and sustainable development. By adhering to principles of responsibility, transparency, and inclusivity, AI technologies like GPT-4 can be harnessed effectively for the greater good, driving innovation and progress in a manner that respects both people and the planet.

Chapter 9: The Future of AI and Online Income

The intersection of AI technologies, particularly GPT-4, with online income generation is rapidly evolving, opening up new horizons and opportunities. This chapter explores the potential future developments in AI and how they might influence the landscape of online income.

9.1 Emerging Trends in AI

9.1.1 Advanced AI Technologies: Discuss the latest advancements in AI technologies beyond GPT-4, including more sophisticated natural language processing, machine learning models, and their potential impact on various industries.

9.1.2 Integration of AI in New Sectors: Explore the expanding integration of AI into diverse sectors such as healthcare, finance, education, and creative industries, and its implications for online income opportunities.

9.2 The Evolution of Online Income Models

9.2.1 New Business Models: Delve into how AI is facilitating new online business models, such as AI-driven marketplaces, personalized product or service offerings, and AI-enhanced freelance opportunities.

9.2.2 Transformation of Traditional Models: Discuss how traditional online income models are being transformed by AI, enhancing efficiency, scalability, and personalization.

9.3 The Role of AI in Future Workspaces

9.3.1 AI and the Gig Economy: Examine how AI is shaping the gig economy, creating new opportunities for freelancers and remote workers in AI development, training, and maintenance.

9.3.2 AI in Corporate Environments: Analyze the implications of AI in corporate settings, including AI-assisted decision-making, automated data analysis, and AI-driven strategy development.

9.4 Ethical and Societal Considerations

9.4.1 Addressing Ethical Challenges: Revisit the ethical challenges posed by advanced AI, including the need for ethical frameworks and guidelines in emerging AI applications.

9.4.2 AI's Impact on Society and Employment: Explore AI's broader impact on society and employment, discussing the balance between technological advancement and job displacement concerns.

9.5 Preparing for the AI-Driven Future

9.5.1 Skills Development and Education: Emphasize the importance of skills development and education in AI and related fields to prepare for future job markets.

9.5.2 Fostering Innovation and Adaptability: Encourage a culture of innovation and adaptability, essential for thriving in an AI-driven economic landscape.

9.6 Anticipating Future Developments

9.6.1 AI and Emerging Technologies: Speculate on how emerging technologies like quantum computing and augmented reality might converge with AI to create novel online income streams.

9.6.2 Long-Term Strategic Planning: Discuss the importance of long-term strategic planning in the context of rapidly evolving AI technologies and market dynamics.

Conclusion

The future of AI and online income is bright and full of potential. By staying informed about emerging trends, adapting to new technologies, and considering ethical and societal impacts, individuals and businesses can position themselves to take full advantage of the opportunities presented by AI advancements. This chapter not only reflects on the future possibilities but also serves as a call to action for proactive preparation and strategic planning in the face of AI evolution.

Anticipating Future Developments in AI

As we look toward the horizon of technological advancements, anticipating future developments in AI is crucial for staying ahead in the rapidly evolving digital landscape. This section explores the potential trajectories and breakthroughs in AI that could significantly impact online income strategies and business models.

9.6.1 Technological Advancements in AI

Beyond GPT-4: Examine potential future iterations and successors to GPT-4, projecting advancements in language processing, problem-solving capabilities, and learning efficiency.

Integration with Other Technologies: Explore the possibility of AI integrating more seamlessly with other cutting-edge technologies like blockchain, Internet of Things (IoT), and augmented reality (AR), creating new applications and opportunities.

9.6.2 AI in Emerging Fields

Expansion into New Domains: Predict the expansion of AI into emerging domains such as personalized medicine, environmental conservation, and space exploration, opening up novel avenues for online income.

AI in Creative Industries: Discuss the evolving role of AI in creative fields, including music, art, and literature, and how it may redefine creativity and content generation.

9.6.3 The Evolution of AI-Enabled Services

Advanced AI Services: Anticipate the development of more sophisticated AI-powered services, offering greater personalization, automation, and efficiency in various sectors.

AI as a Service (AIaaS): Explore the potential growth of AI as a Service platforms, providing accessible, scalable AI solutions for businesses and entrepreneurs.

9.6.4 Societal and Ethical Implications

Impact on Society and Work: Delve into the societal implications of advanced AI, including its impact on employment, privacy, and social interactions.

Evolving Ethical Standards: Discuss how ethical standards and regulations for AI might evolve in response to these new developments, emphasizing the need for ongoing dialogue and policy adaptation.

9.6.5 Preparing for an AI-Driven Future

Skills and Education: Emphasize the importance of education and skill development in AI and related fields to prepare for an AI-dominated future.

Strategic Business Adaptation: Advocate for businesses to adopt flexible, forward-thinking strategies that can adapt to rapid AI advancements and market changes.

Conclusion

Anticipating future developments in AI is not just about understanding technological advancements but also about preparing for their broader impact on society, the economy, and individual livelihoods. By staying informed, adaptable, and ethically vigilant, businesses and individuals can navigate the future of AI with foresight and strategic acumen, leveraging emerging opportunities to create and sustain online income in the evolving digital era.

Preparing for the Next Wave of Innovation

As AI technologies continue to evolve rapidly, preparing for the next wave of innovation is crucial for businesses and individuals looking to capitalize on online income opportunities. This section explores strategies and considerations for staying ahead in the ever-changing landscape of AI and technological advancement.

9.7.1 Staying Informed and Adaptive

Continuous Learning: Emphasize the importance of continuous learning and staying informed about the latest developments in AI and related technologies. Encourage readers to engage with ongoing education, whether through formal courses, online resources, or industry events.

Adaptive Mindset: Foster an adaptive mindset that is open to change and innovation. Highlight the importance of being flexible and willing to pivot strategies in response to new technological trends.

9.7.2 Leveraging Emerging Technologies

Exploring New Technologies: Encourage exploration and experimentation with emerging technologies that complement AI, such as blockchain, quantum computing, or augmented reality, to create innovative online income streams.

Integrating Technologies: Discuss the potential for integrating various technologies with AI to enhance efficiency, create new products or services, and improve customer experiences.

9.7.3 Building a Culture of Innovation

Fostering Creativity: Advocate for creating a culture that encourages creativity and experimentation. Emphasize the value of innovative thinking in leveraging AI for new business models and income opportunities.

Collaborative Ecosystems: Highlight the benefits of collaborative ecosystems, including partnerships between businesses, tech communities, and academic institutions, to foster innovation and share knowledge.

9.7.4 Ethical and Sustainable Innovation

Ethical Considerations: Stress the importance of considering ethical implications when adopting new technologies. Encourage the development of AI in a way that is ethical, responsible, and aligned with societal values.

Sustainable Practices: Advocate for sustainability in innovation, ensuring that technological advancements contribute positively to environmental and social welfare.

9.7.5 Strategic Planning for the Future

Long-Term Vision: Encourage readers to develop a long-term strategic vision that anticipates future technological shifts and prepares for their impact on online income strategies.

Scenario Planning: Suggest engaging in scenario planning to anticipate various future states of the market and technology, allowing businesses and individuals to prepare for different outcomes.

9.7.6 Embracing Change and Uncertainty

Resilience in the Face of Change: Discuss the importance of resilience and agility in an environment of rapid technological change and uncertainty.

Opportunity in Disruption: Frame technological disruption as an opportunity rather than a threat, encouraging readers to seize new opportunities presented by the evolving AI landscape.

Conclusion

Preparing for the next wave of innovation in AI requires a proactive approach, encompassing continuous learning, adaptive strategies, and a culture of creativity and collaboration. By staying informed, ethically aware, and strategically prepared, businesses and individuals can navigate the future of AI and technological advancement, harnessing emerging opportunities to generate online income and drive success in the digital era.

Long-Term Strategies for AI-Driven Success

In an era where AI is reshaping industries and economies, developing long-term strategies is crucial for harnessing its potential for sustained success. This section delves into strategies and approaches for building a lasting and successful AI-driven framework in business and online income generation.

9.8.1 Developing a Vision for AI Integration

Strategic Vision for AI: Encourage readers to develop a clear, strategic vision for AI integration within their businesses or projects. This vision should align with long-term goals and reflect an understanding of AI's potential impact on their specific industry.

Scalable AI Solutions: Advocate for the adoption of scalable AI solutions that can grow and evolve with the business, ensuring long-term viability and adaptability.

9.8.2 Investing in AI Infrastructure and Talent

Building Robust Infrastructure: Discuss the importance of investing in robust AI infrastructure, including hardware, software, and networks, to support AI applications.

Talent Acquisition and Development: Emphasize the need to acquire and develop talent skilled in AI, data science, and related fields. Highlight the importance of continuous training and professional development to keep pace with AI advancements.

9.8.3 Fostering an AI-Innovative Culture

Culture of Innovation: Stress the significance of fostering a culture that values innovation, experimentation, and risk-taking in the context of AI.

Encouraging Cross-Disciplinary Collaboration: Promote cross-disciplinary collaboration and knowledge exchange within organizations to spark creative AI applications and solutions.

9.8.4 Emphasizing Ethical AI Practice

Commitment to Ethical AI: Urge a commitment to ethical AI practices, ensuring that AI is used in ways that are fair, transparent, and beneficial to all stakeholders.

Ongoing Ethical Assessments: Suggest implementing ongoing ethical assessments of AI projects to ensure they adhere to evolving ethical standards and societal expectations.

9.8.5 Leveraging AI for Competitive Advantage

Competitive Analysis through AI: Utilize AI for competitive analysis and market intelligence, staying ahead of industry trends and competitor strategies.

Innovative AI-Driven Products/Services: Encourage the development of innovative AI-driven products or services that offer unique value propositions and set the business apart in the marketplace.

9.8.6 Preparing for AI Disruptions and Challenges

Anticipating Market Disruptions: Highlight the importance of anticipating and preparing for market disruptions caused by AI, adapting business models as necessary.

Risk Management in AI Adoption: Discuss strategies for managing risks associated with AI adoption, including technological, operational, and reputational risks.

Conclusion

Long-term success in an AI-driven world requires a thoughtful, strategic approach. By developing a clear vision, investing in necessary resources, fostering an innovative culture, adhering to ethical standards, leveraging AI for competitive advantage, and preparing for potential disruptions, businesses and individuals can position themselves for enduring success in the dynamic landscape shaped by AI technologies like GPT-4.

Chapter 10: Innovative Money-Making Ideas with GPT-4

10.1 Identifying Lucrative Niches: Using GPT-4 for Market Research

- Explore how GPT-4 can analyze market data and consumer trends to identify lucrative niches and emerging business opportunities.

- Case studies on businesses that successfully identified and capitalized on new market niches using AI-driven insights.

10.2 Creating AI-Powered Digital Products

- Discuss the creation of digital products such as AI-based apps, tools, or platforms, and how GPT-4 can enhance their functionality and appeal.

- Examples of successful AI-powered digital products and the roles GPT-4 played in their development.

10.3 GPT-4 in Freelancing and Consulting Services

- How freelancers and consultants can leverage GPT-4 to offer enhanced services like content creation, data analysis, and strategic planning.

- Practical tips for integrating GPT-4 into freelance or consulting business models to increase value and income.

10.4 Developing AI-Driven Educational Tools and Courses

- The role of GPT-4 in creating personalized educational content, tools, and online courses.

- Insights into monetizing AI-driven educational products and the impact of personalized learning experiences on the education industry.

10.5 Leveraging GPT-4 for Automated Trading and Investments

- Explore the use of GPT-4 in financial markets for automated trading systems, investment analysis, and risk assessment.

- Discuss the potential revenue streams from AI-driven trading and investment advisory services.

10.6 Monetizing AI-Enhanced Content Creation

- Detailed strategies for monetizing AI-enhanced content creation in areas like blogging, video production, and social media.

- Success stories of content creators who have effectively used GPT-4 to generate income.

10.7 Innovative Uses of GPT-4 in Entertainment and Media

- Exploring the use of GPT-4 in scriptwriting, music composition, and other creative processes in the entertainment industry.

- Case studies of how media and entertainment businesses have monetized AI-driven content.

10.8 Harnessing GPT-4 for Business Automation Services

- How businesses can offer AI-driven automation services in areas like customer support, data entry, and process optimization.

- Analysis of the market demand for automation services and the role of GPT-4 in meeting these needs.

10.9 Building AI-Powered Apps and Tools

- Opportunities in developing and monetizing AI-powered applications and tools across various industries.

- Examples of successful AI apps and tools that have generated significant income.

10.10 Collaborations and Partnerships in the AI Ecosystem

- The importance of collaborations and partnerships in the AI ecosystem for mutual growth and income generation.

- Strategies for forming successful partnerships and leveraging collective strengths for income opportunities with AI.

Conclusion This chapter provides a comprehensive guide to innovative and practical ways to generate income using GPT-4. It emphasizes the versatility of GPT-4 across various industries and business models, offering readers insights into harnessing this powerful AI for economic gain.

Identifying Lucrative Niches: Using GPT-4 for Market Research

The ability to identify and capitalize on lucrative niches is crucial for success in today's dynamic market. GPT-4, with its advanced data processing and analysis capabilities, is an invaluable tool for uncovering these opportunities. This section delves into how GPT-4 can be leveraged for effective market research to identify profitable niches.

Understanding Market Dynamics with GPT-4

- Utilize GPT-4 to analyze vast amounts of market data, including consumer trends, industry reports, social media feeds, and competitor activities.

- Learn how GPT-4's deep learning algorithms can identify patterns and insights that might be imperceptible to human analysts, revealing emerging market opportunities.

Techniques for Niche Identification

- Discuss techniques for using GPT-4 to identify niches, such as sentiment analysis to gauge consumer interest in specific topics or products.

- Explore the use of GPT-4 to perform competitive analysis, identifying gaps in the market where consumer needs are not being fully met.

Case Studies: Success with AI-Driven Niche Discovery

- Present real-life case studies where businesses have successfully identified and capitalized on niches using AI-driven market research.

- Analyze how GPT-4's insights led to the development of new products, services, or marketing strategies that effectively targeted these niches.

Applying Predictive Analytics to Forecast Niche Viability

- Leverage GPT-4's predictive analytics to forecast the long-term viability and profitability of identified niches.

- Discuss how businesses can use these forecasts to make informed decisions about resource allocation and strategic planning.

Integrating Consumer Insights for Niche Development

- Use GPT-4 to analyze consumer feedback and behavior, providing deeper insights into specific preferences and pain points.

- Explain how these insights can be used to tailor products or services to better meet the needs of a niche market, thereby increasing market penetration and revenue.

Tools and Resources for GPT-4-Driven Research

- Provide a list of tools and resources that can enhance GPT-4's effectiveness in market research, including data aggregation platforms, analytics software, and visualization tools.

- Offer guidance on how to integrate these tools with GPT-4 to maximize the efficiency and accuracy of niche identification.

Ethical Considerations in Market Research

- Address the ethical considerations of using AI for market research, including data privacy concerns and the responsible use of consumer data.

- Emphasize the importance of adhering to legal and ethical guidelines when conducting AI-driven market research.

Conclusion Identifying lucrative niches using GPT-4 opens a realm of possibilities for businesses seeking to gain a competitive edge. By effectively harnessing the power of AI for market research, businesses can uncover hidden opportunities, tailor their offerings, and strategically position themselves in the market for maximum impact and profitability.

Creating AI-Powered Digital Products

In the digital age, AI-powered products represent a significant frontier for innovation and income generation. This section focuses on how entrepreneurs and businesses can leverage GPT-4 to create digital products that meet market demands and open new revenue streams.

Understanding the Potential of AI in Digital Products

- Begin by exploring the vast potential of AI in enhancing digital products. Explain how GPT-4, with its advanced capabilities, can add value to a range of digital offerings, from apps and software to online platforms and tools.

Identifying Opportunities for AI Integration

- Discuss strategies for identifying opportunities where AI can solve specific problems or enhance user experience in digital products. Emphasize the importance of aligning AI capabilities with user needs and market gaps.

Developing AI-Based Apps and Tools

- Provide a step-by-step guide on developing AI-powered apps and tools, from the ideation phase to development and deployment. Cover essential aspects like choosing the right AI model, integrating GPT-4, and user interface design.

- Highlight the importance of user-centered design in creating AI-based products, ensuring that the end product is intuitive, effective, and meets user expectations.

Case Studies of Successful AI-Powered Products

- Include case studies of successful AI-powered digital products that have made a significant impact in their respective markets. Analyze what made these products successful, including how they utilized AI to address specific user needs.

Monetizing AI-Driven Digital Products

- Explore various monetization strategies for AI-driven digital products, such as subscription models, freemium models, one-time purchases, or ad-supported models. Discuss the pros and cons of each model and how to choose the right one based on the product type and target audience.

Ensuring Quality and Continuous Improvement

- Emphasize the importance of quality assurance in AI-driven products. Discuss the need for continuous testing, user feedback incorporation, and regular updates to keep the product relevant and effective.

Navigating Ethical and Privacy Considerations

- Address ethical considerations in AI product development, particularly issues around user privacy, data security, and AI bias. Offer guidelines on developing AI products responsibly, respecting user privacy, and ensuring data is used ethically.

Future Trends in AI-Powered Digital Products

- Conclude the section by discussing emerging trends in AI-powered digital products. Speculate on future developments in AI technology and how they might open up new possibilities for digital product innovation.

Conclusion Creating AI-powered digital products with GPT-4 offers immense opportunities for entrepreneurs and businesses. By understanding the potential of AI, identifying opportunities for integration, and focusing on user-centric design and ethical considerations, businesses can develop innovative products that not only meet market demands but also open new avenues for income generation.

Freelancing and Consulting Services with GPT-4

The advent of GPT-4 opens a new realm of possibilities for freelancers and consultants. This section explores how these professionals can harness GPT-4 to enhance their services, differentiate themselves in the market, and create new revenue streams.

10.3.1 The Rise of AI in Freelancing and Consulting

- Introduce how AI, especially GPT-4, is transforming the landscape of freelancing and consulting. Discuss the growing demand for AI-enabled services in various industries.

10.3.2 GPT-4 Applications in Freelance Services

- Detail specific applications of GPT-4 in freelance work, such as content creation, data analysis, programming, and design. Provide examples of how GPT-4 can be used to enhance quality, efficiency, and creativity in these services.

10.3.3 Enhancing Consulting Services with GPT-4

- Explore how consultants can use GPT-4 to provide more insightful, data-driven advice to clients. Discuss applications in market analysis, business strategy, IT consulting, and other areas where GPT-4's capabilities can add significant value.

10.3.4 Building a Competitive Edge

- Offer strategies for freelancers and consultants to build a competitive edge with GPT-4, such as specializing in AI-driven solutions or integrating GPT-4 into traditional service offerings to enhance their effectiveness and appeal.

10.3.5 Monetizing AI-Enhanced Services

- Discuss various models for monetizing AI-enhanced freelance and consulting services, including project-based fees, retainer models, and performance-based pricing. Highlight the potential for higher earnings through increased efficiency and unique service offerings.

10.3.6 Marketing AI-Enhanced Freelance Services

- Provide insights on effectively marketing AI-enhanced services. Cover aspects like showcasing AI-driven project successes, leveraging online platforms and social media, and networking in AI-focused communities.

10.3.7 Navigating Ethical and Practical Challenges

- Address the ethical considerations in using AI for freelancing and consulting, such as ensuring transparency with clients and maintaining data privacy. Also, discuss practical challenges like staying updated with AI advancements and managing client expectations.

10.3.8 Preparing for the Future

- Conclude by discussing the importance of continuous learning and adaptation in the rapidly evolving field of AI. Encourage freelancers and consultants to stay informed about the latest developments in AI technologies and market trends.

Conclusion Freelancers and consultants have a unique opportunity to harness GPT-4 to enhance their service offerings, create new business opportunities, and establish themselves as leaders in the AI-driven market. By embracing AI, they can deliver unparalleled value to their clients, opening up new avenues for income and professional growth.

Developing Educational Tools and Courses with GPT-4

The integration of AI into education is transforming the way we teach and learn. GPT-4, with its advanced capabilities, offers exciting opportunities to develop innovative educational tools and courses. This section explores how educators, entrepreneurs, and e-learning professionals can leverage GPT-4 to create impactful educational content and tools.

10.4.1 Revolutionizing E-Learning with AI

- Discuss the transformative impact of AI in the educational sector, particularly in e-learning. Highlight how GPT-4 can be used to create more engaging, personalized, and effective learning experiences.

10.4.2 Designing AI-Enhanced Educational Content

- Explore strategies for using GPT-4 to design educational content, including interactive lessons, personalized learning pathways, and adaptive learning materials. Emphasize the AI's ability to tailor content to individual learning styles and needs.

10.4.3 Creating Interactive Learning Tools

- Detail the development of interactive learning tools using GPT-4, such as AI tutors, language learning apps, and simulation-based learning environments. Discuss how these tools can enhance student engagement and knowledge retention.

10.4.4 Developing AI-Powered Online Courses

- Provide insights into creating AI-powered online courses that offer a dynamic learning experience. Cover aspects such as course structure, content generation, and the integration of interactive AI elements.

10.4.5 Leveraging GPT-4 for Educational Assessment

- Discuss how GPT-4 can be employed for educational assessments, including personalized quizzes, automated grading, and feedback systems. Highlight the potential for AI to provide more objective, comprehensive, and insightful evaluations.

10.4.6 Monetizing AI-Driven Educational Products

- Explore various business models for monetizing AI-driven educational products, such as subscription services, pay-per-course, or freemium models. Offer guidance on pricing strategies and marketing these innovative educational solutions.

10.4.7 Ensuring Quality and Accessibility

- Emphasize the importance of maintaining high-quality, accurate content in AI-driven educational tools and courses. Discuss the need for ensuring accessibility and inclusivity in these educational products.

10.4.8 Addressing Ethical and Privacy Concerns

- Address the ethical considerations in using AI in education, particularly around data privacy and the ethical use of student data. Offer strategies for ensuring that AI-driven educational tools respect user privacy and adhere to ethical standards.

10.4.9 Preparing for Future Educational Trends

- Conclude by discussing future trends in AI-driven education, such as the integration of virtual and augmented reality with AI, and the importance of staying ahead of these trends for continued success and innovation.

Conclusion Developing educational tools and courses with GPT-4 opens up a world of possibilities for enhancing learning experiences. By tapping into the potential of AI, educators and e-learning professionals can create groundbreaking educational products that not only make learning more effective but also more accessible and engaging.

Automated Trading and Investments with GPT-4

The world of finance is increasingly embracing AI for automated trading and investments. GPT-4, with its advanced analytical and predictive capabilities, is at the forefront of this revolution. This section delves into how GPT-4 can be utilized to create sophisticated trading algorithms and investment strategies, opening new avenues for income generation in the financial sector.

10.5.1 Introduction to AI in Financial Markets

- Begin with an overview of how AI is transforming the landscape of trading and investment. Discuss the role of GPT-4 in analyzing market data, predicting trends, and executing trades.

10.5.2 Developing AI-Powered Trading Systems

- Explore the process of developing AI-powered trading systems with GPT-4. Cover key aspects such as data collection, algorithm design, backtesting, and risk management.

- Discuss how GPT-4 can process vast quantities of financial data, including historical price data, financial news, and market indicators, to identify profitable trading opportunities.

10.5.3 Enhancing Investment Strategies with AI

- Detail how GPT-4 can be used to enhance investment strategies. This includes portfolio optimization, asset allocation, and predictive analysis for long-term investments.

- Discuss the integration of GPT-4 into robo-advisors for personalized investment advice and portfolio management.

10.5.4 Risk Management and Compliance

- Emphasize the importance of risk management in AI-driven trading and investment. Discuss how GPT-4 can aid in identifying potential risks and developing strategies to mitigate them.

- Cover compliance aspects, ensuring that AI-driven trading systems adhere to financial regulations and ethical trading practices.

10.5.5 Monetizing AI-Driven Financial Services

- Explore various models for monetizing AI-driven financial services, such as offering AI-powered trading platforms, subscription-based robo-advisory services, or consultancy for financial institutions.

- Discuss the competitive advantages and value propositions that AI-driven financial services offer to clients.

10.5.6 Challenges and Considerations

- Address the challenges associated with AI-driven trading and investments, such as algorithmic biases, market unpredictability, and the need for continuous algorithmic refinement.

- Highlight the importance of a balanced approach that combines AI insights with human expertise and judgment.

10.5.7 Preparing for the Future of AI in Finance

- Conclude by discussing future trends in AI-driven finance, such as the increasing integration of AI in personal finance, the growing importance of alternative data sources, and the potential impact of emerging technologies like blockchain.

Conclusion Automated trading and investments with GPT-4 represent a significant frontier in financial technology. By harnessing the power of AI, individuals and businesses can access sophisticated tools for market analysis, trading execution, and investment strategy, potentially leading to enhanced returns and new income opportunities in the financial sector.

Monetizing AI-Enhanced Content Creation

In an era where content is king, AI-enhanced content creation, particularly with tools like GPT-4, offers new pathways for monetization. This section explores various strategies for monetizing AI-assisted content across different platforms and mediums.

10.6.1 The Edge of AI in Content Creation

- Begin by highlighting the advantages of using GPT-4 in content creation, such as increased efficiency, improved quality, and the ability to generate large volumes of content.

10.6.2 Developing Unique Content Strategies

- Discuss how GPT-4 can be used to develop unique content strategies that cater to specific audience needs, enhance user engagement, and stand out in crowded digital spaces.

10.6.3 Monetizing Written Content

- Explore monetization strategies for AI-generated written content, including blogging, article writing, and ebook creation.

- Cover methods like direct sales, advertising, sponsored content, and subscription models.

10.6.4 Leveraging AI for Video and Podcast Production

- Detail how GPT-4 can assist in scripting and producing video and podcast content. Discuss monetization through platforms like YouTube, Patreon, and podcast advertising networks.

10.6.5 AI in Social Media Management

- Explain how GPT-4 can enhance social media management and content creation. Discuss monetization through influencer marketing, sponsored posts, and social media advertising.

10.6.6 Creating Educational and Training Materials

- Discuss the creation and monetization of educational and training materials using GPT-4, such as online courses, webinars, and instructional guides.

10.6.7 Selling AI-Generated Art and Creative Works

- Delve into the world of AI-generated art, music, and other creative works. Discuss platforms and marketplaces for selling these creations and how to price them.

10.6.8 Subscription Models and Membership Sites

- Explore the potential of subscription models and membership sites for regular income from AI-enhanced content. Discuss how to build and maintain a loyal subscriber base.

10.6.9 Challenges and Ethical Considerations

- Address challenges such as ensuring originality in AI-generated content and navigating copyright issues.

- Discuss ethical considerations in disclosing AI use in content creation and maintaining transparency with audiences.

10.6.10 Future Trends in AI Content Monetization

- Conclude with a look at potential future trends in AI content creation and monetization, including emerging platforms and evolving consumer preferences.

Conclusion AI-enhanced content creation offers a multitude of opportunities for monetization in today's digital landscape. From traditional blogging to innovative AI-generated art, GPT-4 can be a powerful tool in a content creator's arsenal, enabling the creation of diverse, high-quality content that can be monetized through various channels.

Uses in Entertainment and Media with GPT-4

The entertainment and media industry is undergoing a significant transformation with the advent of AI technologies like GPT-4. This section explores how GPT-4 is being used to create innovative content, enhance user experiences, and open new revenue streams in entertainment and media.

10.7.1 Revolutionizing Content Creation

- Discuss how GPT-4 is used to create novel content in entertainment and media, including scriptwriting, music composition, and interactive storytelling. Highlight its ability to generate creative, engaging narratives and dialogue.

10.7.2 Enhancing Film and Television Production

- Explore the use of GPT-4 in film and television production, from conceptualization and script development to post-production processes. Discuss how AI can assist in creating more nuanced and complex plots.

10.7.3 Transforming Music and Audio Production

- Delve into GPT-4's role in music production, including composition, lyric writing, and sound design. Highlight how AI is enabling the creation of new music genres and experimental sounds.

10.7.4 Innovating in Gaming and Interactive Media

- Detail the application of GPT-4 in gaming and interactive media, such as developing dynamic game narratives, character dialogue, and responsive storytelling elements that adapt to player choices.

10.7.5 AI in Journalism and Publishing

- Discuss the use of GPT-4 in journalism and publishing, including automated news reporting, data journalism, and personalized content curation for readers.

10.7.6 Monetizing AI-Driven Entertainment and Media

- Explore various business models for monetizing AI-driven projects in entertainment and media, such as direct sales, subscription services, advertising, and licensing deals.

10.7.7 Collaborative Art and Crowdsourced Projects

- Highlight GPT-4's role in collaborative art projects and crowdsourced media content, discussing how AI is used to amalgamate diverse ideas and creative inputs from a global audience.

10.7.8 Addressing Ethical and Copyright Concerns

- Address ethical considerations and copyright issues in AI-generated content. Discuss the importance of maintaining transparency, crediting AI contributions, and navigating the legal landscape of AI-created works.

10.7.9 Leveraging AI for Marketing and Promotion

- Explain how GPT-4 can be used in marketing and promotion within the entertainment and media sector, including personalized advertising, audience analysis, and content recommendation algorithms.

10.7.10 Future Trends and Potential Developments

- Conclude by speculating on future trends in AI's role in entertainment and media. Discuss potential developments and how they might further reshape these industries.

Conclusion GPT-4's integration into entertainment and media is opening up a new realm of possibilities, from AI-scripted films to algorithmically composed music. This technological evolution not only enhances the creative process but also offers new avenues for monetization and audience engagement in the digital era.

Business Automation Services with GPT-4

In the current business landscape, efficiency and innovation are key drivers of success. GPT-4's capabilities in business automation offer transformative solutions. This section explores how businesses can leverage GPT-4 for automation services to streamline operations, reduce costs, and enhance productivity.

10.8.1 The Role of GPT-4 in Business Automation

- Introduce how GPT-4 is revolutionizing business automation. Highlight its ability to process and analyze large volumes of data, automate routine tasks, and provide intelligent insights for decision-making.

10.8.2 Automating Administrative Tasks

- Discuss the use of GPT-4 in automating administrative tasks such as scheduling, email management, and documentation. Explain how automating these tasks can free up valuable time and resources for businesses.

10.8.3 Enhancing Customer Service and Support

- Explore the application of GPT-4 in enhancing customer service. Include examples such as AI-driven chatbots for customer inquiries, automated helpdesk support, and personalized customer communication.

10.8.4 Streamlining Financial Operations

- Detail how GPT-4 can be used to streamline financial operations, including automated invoicing, expense tracking, and financial reporting. Discuss the accuracy and efficiency gains from using AI in finance.

10.8.5 Optimizing Supply Chain and Logistics

- Examine the role of GPT-4 in optimizing supply chain and logistics. Cover areas such as demand forecasting, inventory management, and logistics planning.

10.8.6 Implementing AI in Marketing and Sales

- Discuss the use of GPT-4 in automating various aspects of marketing and sales, such as data-driven market analysis, personalized marketing content, and sales forecasting.

10.8.7 Monetizing Business Automation Services

- Explore different business models for monetizing GPT-4-powered automation services. Discuss strategies such as offering AI-as-a-Service (AIaaS), subscription models, or custom AI solution development for clients.

10.8.8 Navigating Challenges in AI Automation

- Address the challenges and considerations in implementing AI automation, including integration with existing systems, ensuring data security, and managing change within organizations.

10.8.9 Ethical Considerations in AI Deployment

- Highlight the ethical considerations in deploying AI for business automation, such as transparency, privacy concerns, and the potential impact on employment.

10.8.10 Preparing Businesses for AI Integration

- Offer guidance on preparing businesses for AI integration. Include aspects such as assessing business needs, upskilling employees, and establishing a framework for ongoing AI management and adaptation.

Conclusion Integrating GPT-4 into business automation services presents a significant opportunity for businesses to enhance operational efficiency and drive growth. By embracing AI, businesses can not only streamline their operations but also open new avenues for innovation and revenue generation in the digital age.

Building AI-Powered Apps and Tools with GPT-4

The development of AI-powered apps and tools is a rapidly growing field, offering immense potential for innovation and profitability. GPT-4, with its advanced capabilities, provides a solid foundation for creating applications that can revolutionize various industries. This section explores the process and potential of building AI-powered apps and tools using GPT-4.

10.9.1 Identifying Market Opportunities for AI Apps

- Discuss how to identify market needs and opportunities for AI-powered applications. Emphasize the importance of market research and understanding customer pain points that AI can address.

10.9.2 Designing and Developing AI Solutions

- Offer insights into the design and development process of AI-powered apps and tools. Cover key steps such as conceptualizing the solution, integrating GPT-4 for specific functionalities, and user interface design.

- Highlight the importance of a user-centric approach in designing AI apps, ensuring they are intuitive, effective, and cater to the target audience's needs.

10.9.3 Innovative Use Cases of GPT-4 in App Development

- Present innovative use cases of GPT-4 in various domains such as healthcare, education, finance, and customer service. Include examples of apps that have successfully leveraged GPT-4 to offer unique solutions.

10.9.4 Ensuring Quality and Performance

- Discuss strategies for ensuring the quality and performance of AI-powered apps. Emphasize the need for thorough testing, user feedback incorporation, and continuous improvement based on real-world usage.

10.9.5 Monetization Strategies for AI Apps

- Explore various monetization strategies for AI-powered apps, including subscription models, in-app purchases, freemium models, and advertising. Offer guidance on choosing the right monetization strategy based on the app's functionality and target audience.

10.9.6 Marketing and Promoting AI Tools

- Provide tips on effectively marketing and promoting AI-powered tools. Discuss the use of digital marketing strategies, leveraging social media, content marketing, and partnerships to increase app visibility and adoption.

10.9.7 Addressing Ethical and Privacy Concerns

- Highlight the ethical considerations in AI app development, particularly around data privacy, security, and AI bias. Offer best practices for developing AI tools that are ethical and compliant with data protection regulations.

10.9.8 Navigating Challenges in AI App Development

- Address common challenges in AI app development, including technical complexities, integration with existing systems, and keeping up with rapidly evolving AI technologies.

10.9.9 Preparing for Future AI Advancements

- Conclude by discussing the need to stay informed about future advancements in AI and GPT-4. Emphasize the importance of adaptability and continuous learning to ensure AI apps remain relevant and competitive.

Conclusion Building AI-powered apps and tools with GPT-4 is a venture that combines creativity, technical skill, and market insight. By harnessing the capabilities of GPT-4, developers and entrepreneurs can create innovative solutions that not only meet current market demands but also pave the way for future technological advancements.

Collaborations and Partnerships in the AI Ecosystem

The AI ecosystem thrives on collaborations and partnerships, bringing together diverse expertise and resources for mutual benefit. This section examines how strategic collaborations and partnerships can be formed and leveraged in the AI space, particularly with GPT-4, to foster innovation, expand market reach, and create lucrative opportunities.

10.10.1 The Value of Collaborative Efforts in AI

- Start with an overview of why collaborations and partnerships are particularly valuable in the AI field. Highlight the benefits of combining different skill sets, perspectives, and resources to enhance AI development and application.

10.10.2 Identifying Potential Partners

- Discuss strategies for identifying potential partners in the AI space. This includes looking for complementary skills, shared goals, and synergistic opportunities in industries ranging from technology and healthcare to finance and education.

10.10.3 Forming Strategic AI Partnerships

- Offer guidance on forming strategic partnerships. Cover aspects such as establishing common goals, defining roles and responsibilities, and setting clear expectations for collaboration.

10.10.4 Collaborating on AI Research and Development

- Delve into collaborations specifically focused on AI research and development. Discuss how partnerships can facilitate innovative research, share the burden of development costs, and accelerate the time to market for new AI solutions.

10.10.5 Joint Ventures in AI-Powered Product Development

- Explore the potential for joint ventures in developing AI-powered products and services. Include examples of successful joint ventures and how they have capitalized on the strengths of each partner.

10.10.6 Leveraging Partnerships for Market Expansion

- Discuss how collaborations and partnerships can be leveraged for market expansion. This includes accessing new customer bases, leveraging partner networks, and enhancing product offerings with complementary technologies.

10.10.7 Navigating Legal and Ethical Considerations

- Address the legal and ethical considerations in AI partnerships, such as intellectual property rights, data sharing agreements, and compliance with AI ethics and regulations.

10.10.8 Building Long-Term Collaborative Relationships

- Provide insights into building and maintaining long-term collaborative relationships in the AI ecosystem. Emphasize the importance of trust, communication, and a shared vision for success.

10.10.9 Case Studies of Successful AI Collaborations

- Include case studies of successful AI collaborations and partnerships, highlighting key lessons learned, challenges overcome, and the impact of these collaborations.

Conclusion Collaborations and partnerships in the AI ecosystem are powerful mechanisms for driving innovation, accelerating growth, and achieving success. By strategically aligning with the right partners and fostering collaborative relationships, businesses and individuals can tap into the collective potential of AI technologies like GPT-4, unlocking new opportunities and pathways for revenue generation.

Chapter 11: AI and Real Estate Investing

The integration of Artificial Intelligence (AI) into real estate investing is transforming the industry, making processes more efficient and investments more lucrative. GPT-4, with its advanced capabilities, plays a significant role in this transformation. This chapter explores the numerous applications of AI in real estate investing.

11.1 The Intersection of AI and Real Estate

- Introduce how AI, specifically GPT-4, is changing the landscape of real estate investing. Cover its impact on market analysis, property valuation, investment decision-making, and customer service.

11.2 Utilizing GPT-4 for Market Analysis and Trends

- Discuss how GPT-4 can be used to analyze real estate markets, identifying trends, growth areas, and potential investment opportunities. Explain how AI-driven analytics can process vast amounts of data to provide comprehensive market insights.

11.3 Enhancing Property Valuation with AI

- Explore the use of GPT-4 in property valuation. Delve into how AI algorithms can accurately assess property values by considering numerous factors, including location, historical data, market trends, and property features.

11.4 AI in Property Management and Operations

- Detail the application of GPT-4 in property management, including automated tenant screening, maintenance scheduling, and rent collection. Discuss how AI can optimize operational efficiency and improve tenant relations.

11.5 AI-Driven Marketing Strategies for Real Estate

- Examine how AI, especially GPT-4, is revolutionizing real estate marketing. Cover topics such as targeted advertising, automated content creation for listings, and personalized customer engagement.

11.6 Personalized Real Estate Services with AI

- Discuss the role of GPT-4 in providing personalized real estate services, such as matching buyers with ideal properties based on their preferences and behavior analysis.

11.7 AI in Real Estate Investment Analysis

- Explore how investors are using GPT-4 for investment analysis, including ROI estimation, risk assessment, and portfolio diversification. Discuss how AI enhances the decision-making process with predictive analytics.

11.8 Ethical Considerations and Data Privacy in AI-Driven Real Estate

- Address the ethical considerations and data privacy issues in the use of AI in real estate. Highlight the importance of ethical AI practices, data security, and compliance with privacy laws.

11.9 Case Studies: Success Stories in AI-Enabled Real Estate

- Present real-world case studies where AI, particularly GPT-4, has been successfully applied in real estate investing, resulting in significant returns and market advantages.

11.10 Preparing for the Future of AI in Real Estate Investing

- Conclude the chapter by discussing the future potential of AI in real estate. Highlight upcoming trends, potential technological advancements, and how investors can prepare for and adapt to these changes.

Conclusion AI, and specifically GPT-4, offers groundbreaking opportunities in real estate investing. From enhancing market analysis to optimizing property management and improving investment strategies, AI is set to redefine the industry. Investors who embrace these AI-driven tools and methodologies are well-positioned to gain a significant competitive edge.

The Intersection of AI and Real Estate

The real estate industry is experiencing a paradigm shift with the integration of Artificial Intelligence (AI), particularly with advanced tools like GPT-4. This section delves into how AI is reshaping various aspects of real estate, from property search and transactions to investment and management.

Understanding the AI Revolution in Real Estate

- Start by providing an overview of how AI is revolutionizing the real estate sector. Discuss the growing trend of using AI tools like GPT-4 for data analysis, predictive modeling, and automation in real estate processes.

AI-Driven Market Analysis and Prediction

- Highlight the role of AI in real estate market analysis. Detail how GPT-4 can analyze vast datasets to identify market trends, predict property value fluctuations, and suggest optimal times for buying or selling properties.

Enhancing Property Search and Recommendations

- Discuss the application of AI in improving property search platforms. Explain how GPT-4 can personalize property recommendations based on individual user preferences, search history, and market data.

Streamlining Real Estate Transactions

- Explore how AI streamlines real estate transactions. Cover areas such as automated document processing, AI-driven due diligence, and virtual property tours, which significantly enhance the efficiency and speed of transactions.

Predictive Maintenance and Property Management

- Delve into the role of AI in predictive maintenance and property management. Discuss how AI tools can forecast maintenance needs, optimize property operations, and enhance tenant experiences.

AI in Real Estate Investment Strategies

- Detail the use of AI in shaping real estate investment strategies. Explain how tools like GPT-4 assist investors in identifying profitable investment opportunities, assessing risk, and making data-driven investment decisions.

The Future of Real Estate Development with AI

- Speculate on the future role of AI in real estate development. Cover potential advancements such as AI-driven urban planning, smart building technologies, and the development of sustainable, AI-integrated living spaces.

Challenges and Opportunities

- Address the challenges of integrating AI into real estate, including data privacy concerns, the need for accurate and unbiased data, and the importance of combining AI insights with human expertise.

- Highlight the opportunities AI presents in transforming the real estate industry, making it more efficient, customer-friendly, and profitable.

Conclusion The intersection of AI and real estate signifies a transformative era in the industry. AI tools like GPT-4 are not only streamlining operations but also opening new avenues for investment, development, and customer engagement. As AI continues to evolve, its impact on the real estate sector promises to be profound and far-reaching.

Utilizing GPT-4 for Market Analysis and Trends in Real Estate

The real estate market is dynamic and complex, with a constant influx of data from various sources. GPT-4's advanced capabilities make it an invaluable tool for analyzing this data and identifying market trends.

This section explores how GPT-4 can be leveraged for insightful market analysis in real estate.

11.2.1 Harnessing GPT-4 for Comprehensive Market Insights

- Begin by discussing how GPT-4 can process and analyze vast amounts of real estate data, including market reports, property listings, transaction histories, and economic indicators.

- Explain how GPT-4's ability to understand and interpret natural language allows it to extract insights from varied data sources, including news articles and social media, providing a holistic view of the market.

11.2.2 Identifying Emerging Trends and Patterns

- Detail how GPT-4 can identify emerging trends and patterns in the real estate market. This includes spotting shifts in property prices, changes in consumer preferences, and emerging hotspots for investment.

- Discuss how GPT-4's predictive analytics capabilities can forecast future market movements, aiding investors and professionals in making informed decisions.

11.2.3 Customized Market Analysis Reports

- Explore the potential of GPT-4 to generate customized market analysis reports tailored to specific requirements, such as focusing on a particular geographic area, property type, or investment range.

- Highlight how these AI-generated reports can save time and resources while providing in-depth and up-to-date market insights.

11.2.4 Enhancing Investment Decision-Making

- Discuss how GPT-4's market analysis can enhance real estate investment decision-making. Cover how AI-driven insights can help in assessing the viability of investments, understanding risk factors, and identifying optimal investment timing.

11.2.5 Integrating AI with Traditional Market Research

- Emphasize the importance of integrating AI-driven insights with traditional market research methods. Discuss how a combined approach can provide a more comprehensive and accurate market analysis.

11.2.6 Overcoming Challenges in AI-Driven Analysis

- Address potential challenges in using AI for market analysis, such as data accuracy, bias in AI algorithms, and the need for human oversight to interpret AI-generated insights correctly.

11.2.7 Preparing for AI-Driven Market Changes

- Conclude by preparing real estate professionals for the AI-driven changes in market analysis. Emphasize the need for continuous learning and adaptation to leverage AI tools effectively in the ever-evolving real estate landscape.

Conclusion Utilizing GPT-4 for market analysis in real estate offers unparalleled advantages. Its ability to process vast datasets and identify trends can significantly enhance market understanding and inform smarter investment strategies. As AI technology continues to evolve, its role in shaping real estate market analysis and trend prediction is set to grow exponentially.

Enhancing Property Valuation with AI

Accurate property valuation is a cornerstone of successful real estate investing. The advent of AI, particularly GPT-4, has revolutionized property valuation processes, making them more accurate, efficient, and data-driven. This section explores how AI can enhance property valuation in the real estate market.

11.3.1 AI-Driven Approaches to Property Valuation

- Introduce the concept of AI-driven property valuation, explaining how GPT-4 and related technologies can analyze vast datasets to estimate property values more accurately than traditional methods.

- Discuss the types of data AI can process for valuation, including historical sales data, current market trends, property features, location specifics, and economic indicators.

11.3.2 Advantages of AI in Valuation Accuracy

- Highlight the increased accuracy offered by AI in property valuation. Discuss how AI algorithms can detect nuances and patterns in data that might be overlooked in manual appraisals.

- Cover the speed and efficiency of AI-driven valuations, emphasizing how they can process large volumes of data quickly to provide real-time property value estimates.

11.3.3 Predictive Analytics in Property Valuation

- Explore the use of predictive analytics in AI for future property valuation. Discuss how GPT-4 can forecast future market changes and property value fluctuations based on current data trends and predictive modeling.

11.3.4 Customized Valuation Reports

- Detail how AI can generate customized valuation reports tailored to specific investor needs or property types. Discuss the flexibility and scalability of AI in providing detailed reports for diverse property portfolios.

11.3.5 Integrating AI with Traditional Valuation Methods

- Discuss the importance of integrating AI-driven valuation with traditional methods. Highlight how a combined approach ensures comprehensive valuation by leveraging the strengths of both AI and human expertise.

11.3.6 Challenges and Limitations of AI in Valuation

- Address the challenges and limitations of using AI in property valuation, such as the need for high-quality data, potential biases in AI models, and the importance of human oversight in interpreting AI-generated valuations.

11.3.7 Preparing for an AI-Enhanced Valuation Future

- Conclude by preparing real estate professionals and investors for the future of AI-enhanced property valuation. Emphasize the need for adapting to AI-driven processes and the importance of staying informed about AI advancements in real estate.

Conclusion AI, particularly GPT-4, is transforming property valuation in real estate. By providing accurate, efficient, and data-driven valuations, AI enhances the decision-making process for investors and professionals. As AI technology continues to advance, its role in property valuation is set to become even more integral, offering new levels of insight and efficiency in the real estate market.

AI in Property Management

Incorporating AI into property management is revolutionizing the way properties are managed, maintained, and optimized for profitability. This section delves into how AI, especially GPT-4, is being utilized to enhance various facets of property management.

11.4.1 Transforming Property Management with AI

- Introduce the role of AI in modern property management. Explain how AI, particularly GPT-4, is being used to automate and optimize various management tasks, from tenant screening to maintenance scheduling.

11.4.2 Automating Tenant Communication and Services

- Discuss how AI can automate and improve tenant communication. Highlight AI-driven chatbots for tenant queries, automated alerts and notifications, and AI-enhanced customer service platforms.

11.4.3 Enhancing Maintenance and Operations

- Detail the use of AI in predictive maintenance, where AI algorithms analyze data from sensors and IoT devices to predict and schedule maintenance tasks proactively.

- Explore the role of AI in optimizing building operations, including energy management, security surveillance, and facility management.

11.4.4 Streamlining Administrative Tasks

- Examine how AI can streamline administrative tasks in property management. Cover aspects such as lease processing, rent collection automation, and financial reporting.

11.4.5 AI-Driven Market Analysis for Property Managers

- Discuss how property managers can use AI for market analysis, including tracking rental market trends, benchmarking property performance, and making data-driven decisions to maximize returns.

11.4.6 Enhancing Tenant Experience and Retention

- Highlight how AI can be used to enhance the tenant experience, leading to higher tenant satisfaction and retention. Discuss personalized tenant services, AI-driven amenities recommendations, and community engagement tools.

11.4.7 Challenges and Considerations in AI Implementation

- Address the challenges of implementing AI in property management, such as integration with existing systems, data privacy concerns, and the need for human oversight.

11.4.8 Future Trends in AI-Driven Property Management

- Conclude by exploring future trends in AI-driven property management. Speculate on upcoming advancements in AI technology and how they might further transform property management practices.

Conclusion AI, particularly GPT-4, offers property managers a powerful tool to enhance efficiency, improve tenant satisfaction, and optimize property performance. As AI technology continues to evolve, its impact on property management is expected to grow, offering new opportunities for innovation in the real estate industry.

AI-Driven Marketing in Real Estate

The real estate industry is increasingly leveraging AI-driven marketing to reach potential clients more effectively and efficiently. This section explores how GPT-4 and other AI tools are transforming real estate marketing strategies.

11.5.1 Revolutionizing Real Estate Marketing with AI

- Introduce the concept of AI-driven marketing in real estate. Highlight how GPT-4 and other AI technologies are enabling more targeted, personalized, and efficient marketing strategies.

11.5.2 Personalized Property Recommendations

- Discuss how AI algorithms, including GPT-4, can analyze customer data and behavior to provide personalized property recommendations. Explain how this leads to higher engagement and conversion rates.

11.5.3 Automating Marketing Content Creation

- Explore the role of AI in automating marketing content creation. Cover areas such as AI-generated property descriptions, automated social media posts, and email marketing campaigns tailored to individual client preferences.

11.5.4 Enhancing Customer Engagement and Lead Generation

- Detail how AI tools can enhance customer engagement and lead generation. Discuss AI-driven chatbots for instant customer interaction, lead qualification, and nurturing.

11.5.5 Data-Driven Market Analysis for Targeted Advertising

- Examine how AI can be used for data-driven market analysis, enabling highly targeted advertising campaigns. Highlight the ability of AI to identify and segment target audiences, optimize ad placement, and track campaign performance.

11.5.6 AI in Virtual Property Tours and Showings

- Discuss the integration of AI with virtual reality (VR) and augmented reality (AR) for creating immersive virtual property tours and showings. Explain how this technology can attract and engage prospective buyers or tenants.

11.5.7 Measuring and Optimizing Marketing ROI with AI

- Cover the use of AI in measuring and optimizing the return on investment (ROI) of marketing campaigns. Discuss how AI analytics can provide insights into campaign effectiveness and suggest adjustments for improved results.

11.5.8 Ethical Considerations in AI-Driven Marketing

- Address the ethical considerations in AI-driven marketing, including concerns about data privacy, transparency in AI decision-making, and avoiding bias in targeting and recommendations.

11.5.9 Preparing for an AI-Enhanced Marketing Future

- Conclude by preparing real estate professionals for the future of AI-enhanced marketing. Emphasize the importance of staying informed about AI advancements and adapting marketing strategies accordingly.

Conclusion AI-driven marketing is reshaping the way real estate businesses connect with clients and market properties. By adopting AI tools like GPT-4, real estate professionals can benefit from more efficient, effective, and personalized marketing strategies, leading to increased client engagement and business growth.

Personalized Real Estate Services with AI

The personalization of real estate services using AI, especially GPT-4, is redefining customer experiences in the industry. This section explores how AI can be utilized to deliver tailored real estate services, enhancing customer satisfaction and driving business growth.

11.6.1 Tailoring Customer Experiences in Real Estate

- Discuss the importance of personalized experiences in today's real estate market. Explain how AI, particularly GPT-4, enables customization of services based on individual client preferences, behavior, and needs.

11.6.2 AI-Enhanced Property Matching

- Detail the role of AI in enhancing property matching. Describe how GPT-4 can analyze client profiles, preferences, and past interactions to recommend properties that closely match their requirements.

11.6.3 Customized Communication and Interaction

- Explore how AI can tailor communication with clients. Cover aspects such as AI-driven chatbots providing personalized responses, automated follow-ups, and AI-enabled CRM systems that track client preferences for more meaningful interactions.

11.6.4 Personalized Market Reports and Insights

- Discuss how AI can generate personalized market reports and insights for clients. Explain how GPT-4 can analyze market data and trends to provide clients with customized information relevant to their investment goals or property interests.

11.6.5 Optimizing the Buyer and Seller Journey

- Examine how AI can optimize the buyer and seller journey in real estate. Discuss how AI tools can guide clients through the process, from initial inquiry and property viewing to transaction completion, based on their unique preferences and timelines.

11.6.6 AI-Driven Virtual Consultations and Tours

- Highlight the use of AI in virtual consultations and tours. Discuss how AI can facilitate virtual property showings that are tailored to highlight features of interest to specific clients.

11.6.7 Enhancing Post-Sale and Property Management Services

- Cover the application of AI in post-sale services and property management. Discuss how AI can provide personalized recommendations for property maintenance, upgrades, and management based on client preferences and property specifics.

11.6.8 Addressing Challenges in Personalized AI Services

- Address the challenges of implementing personalized AI services in real estate, such as ensuring accuracy in AI recommendations, maintaining data privacy, and balancing AI-driven services with a human touch.

11.6.9 Future Trends in AI-Powered Personalization

- Conclude by discussing future trends in AI-powered personalization in real estate. Speculate on how ongoing advancements in AI technology may further enhance personalized real estate services.

Conclusion The use of AI in providing personalized real estate services represents a significant advancement in enhancing client experiences and service efficiency. As AI technologies like GPT-4 continue to evolve, they offer real estate professionals new opportunities to deliver highly customized, client-centric services, setting a new standard in the industry.

AI in Real Estate Investment Analysis

In the realm of real estate investment, the analytical power of AI, especially tools like GPT-4, is becoming increasingly indispensable. This section explores how AI is reshaping investment analysis, offering more sophisticated, data-driven insights for investors.

11.7.1 The Impact of AI on Investment Decision-Making

- Begin with an overview of how AI is transforming real estate investment decision-making. Highlight how GPT-4's advanced data processing capabilities enable deeper market insights and more informed investment choices.

11.7.2 AI-Driven Market and Risk Analysis

- Discuss the role of AI in conducting comprehensive market analysis. Cover how GPT-4 can analyze market trends, economic indicators, and demographic data to assess investment risks and opportunities.

- Explore how AI models can predict market fluctuations, helping investors to strategize and mitigate risks.

11.7.3 Enhancing Property Portfolio Management

- Detail the application of AI in managing property portfolios. Discuss how AI tools can optimize portfolio performance by recommending buy, hold, or sell decisions based on real-time market data and predictive analytics.

11.7.4 Customized Investment Strategies with AI

- Explain how AI enables the creation of customized investment strategies. Describe how GPT-4 can consider an investor's specific goals, risk tolerance, and investment preferences to suggest tailored investment approaches.

11.7.5 AI in Due Diligence and Property Valuation

- Highlight the importance of AI in conducting due diligence and property valuation. Discuss how AI can rapidly analyze legal documents, property history, and financial records to provide comprehensive property valuations.

11.7.6 Predictive Analytics in Project Development

- Cover the use of predictive analytics in real estate project development. Discuss how AI can forecast project outcomes, return on investment (ROI), and the long-term viability of development projects.

11.7.7 Challenges and Ethical Considerations

- Address the challenges and ethical considerations in using AI for investment analysis, including the accuracy of data, potential biases in AI models, and the need for responsible data handling and privacy.

11.7.8 Preparing for an AI-Enhanced Investment Future

- Conclude by preparing investors for an AI-enhanced future in real estate investment. Emphasize the importance of staying abreast of AI advancements and integrating AI tools into investment analysis practices.

Conclusion AI, particularly GPT-4, offers groundbreaking tools for real estate investment analysis, enabling investors to make more informed, data-driven decisions. As AI technologies continue to evolve, their role in enhancing investment strategies and portfolio management is set to grow, providing investors with a significant competitive edge in the real estate market.

Ethical Considerations in AI-Driven Real Estate

As AI, particularly GPT-4, becomes more integrated into the real estate industry, it's crucial to address the ethical considerations that arise. This section explores the ethical implications of using AI in real estate and offers guidance on navigating these challenges responsibly.

11.8.1 The Importance of Ethical AI Practices

- Start by emphasizing the importance of ethical practices in AI-driven real estate. Highlight how ethical considerations impact trust, reputation, and compliance in the industry.

11.8.2 Addressing Bias and Fairness in AI Algorithms

- Discuss the issue of bias in AI algorithms. Explain how biases in data or programming can lead to unfair or discriminatory outcomes in areas such as property valuations, tenant screening, or targeted marketing.

- Offer strategies for identifying and mitigating these biases to ensure fairness and equality in AI-driven processes.

11.8.3 Data Privacy and Security

- Examine the critical importance of data privacy and security in AI-driven real estate operations. Discuss the need to protect sensitive client and property data, and comply with data protection regulations like GDPR or CCPA.

- Provide best practices for maintaining data privacy and security, including transparent data usage policies and robust cybersecurity measures.

11.8.4 Transparency and Accountability in AI Decisions

- Highlight the need for transparency and accountability in AI-driven decision-making processes. Discuss how real estate professionals can ensure that AI decisions are understandable, traceable, and accountable.

- Explain the role of explainable AI (XAI) in making AI processes more transparent and understandable to clients and stakeholders.

11.8.5 Ethical Considerations in AI-Driven Marketing

- Address the ethical considerations specific to AI-driven marketing in real estate. Cover issues such as personalized

131

advertising, data-driven profiling, and respecting consumer privacy and consent.

11.8.6 The Impact of AI on Employment

- Discuss the impact of AI on employment within the real estate sector. Cover the importance of balancing AI integration with job preservation and the need for upskilling and reskilling workers to work alongside AI technologies.

11.8.7 Developing Ethical AI Policies

- Provide guidance on developing and implementing ethical AI policies in real estate businesses. Emphasize the importance of stakeholder engagement, continuous review, and adaptation of these policies to evolving standards and technologies.

11.8.8 Navigating Legal and Ethical Landscapes

- Conclude by discussing the need to navigate the evolving legal and ethical landscapes in AI-driven real estate. Emphasize staying informed about legal changes, engaging with ethical AI communities, and advocating for responsible AI practices.

Conclusion Ethical considerations in AI-driven real estate are paramount to the responsible and sustainable integration of AI technologies in the industry. By addressing issues such as bias, data privacy, transparency, and employment impacts, real estate professionals can harness the benefits of AI while upholding ethical standards and building trust with clients and the broader community.

Case Studies: Success Stories in AI-Enabled Real Estate

Real-world examples can powerfully illustrate the transformative impact of AI in real estate. This section presents a series of case studies highlighting successful applications of AI technologies, including GPT-4, in various aspects of the real estate industry.

11.9.1 AI-Driven Property Valuation: A Tech Startup's Breakthrough

- Present a case study of a tech startup that utilized AI for property valuation. Discuss how the company leveraged AI algorithms to analyze market data and accurately assess property values, leading to a significant increase in efficiency and accuracy over traditional methods.

11.9.2 Revolutionizing Real Estate Marketing with AI

- Detail the story of a real estate agency that implemented AI-driven marketing strategies. Cover how they used AI for targeted advertising, personalized content creation, and predictive analytics to understand customer preferences, resulting in increased sales and customer engagement.

11.9.3 AI-Powered Investment Analysis: Transforming Portfolio Management

- Showcase a real estate investment firm that adopted AI for investment analysis. Explain how they used AI tools to evaluate market trends, forecast investment returns, and optimize their property portfolio, achieving higher returns and risk mitigation.

11.9.4 Enhancing Customer Service with AI Chatbots

- Introduce a case where a property management company implemented AI chatbots. Discuss how the chatbots provided instant, personalized responses to tenant queries, improving customer service and operational efficiency.

11.9.5 Automating Administrative Processes in Property Management

- Describe how a property management company automated its administrative processes using AI. Highlight the impact of AI on improving lease processing, rent collection, and maintenance scheduling.

11.9.6 Predictive Maintenance: A Game-Changer for Property Managers

- Offer an example of a property management firm that utilized AI for predictive maintenance. Discuss how AI predictive models helped them anticipate maintenance needs, reducing costs and enhancing property upkeep.

11.9.7 AI-Enabled Urban Development Projects

- Present a case study of an urban development project where AI was used for planning and development. Highlight how AI analyzed demographic data, traffic patterns, and environmental factors to inform sustainable and efficient urban design.

11.9.8 Overcoming Challenges: A Real Estate Company's Journey

- Share a story of a real estate company that faced and overcame challenges in implementing AI. Cover the obstacles they encountered, such as data integration issues and employee training, and how they successfully navigated these challenges.

Conclusion These case studies demonstrate the diverse and impactful ways in which AI, including GPT-4, is being applied in the real estate industry. From enhancing property valuations and marketing strategies to revolutionizing investment analysis and property management, AI is driving significant advancements and successes in the field.

Future of AI in Real Estate Investing

As we look toward the future, the intersection of AI and real estate investing is poised for even more groundbreaking developments. This section speculates on the future trajectory of AI, particularly GPT-4, in the real estate sector and its potential to further revolutionize real estate investing.

11.10.1 Advancements in AI Technology

- Begin by discussing anticipated advancements in AI technology, including more sophisticated machine learning algorithms, improved natural language processing, and enhanced predictive analytics capabilities.

- Speculate on how these advancements could lead to more accurate market predictions, deeper insights into consumer behavior, and more efficient real estate transaction processes.

11.10.2 Integration with Emerging Technologies

- Explore the potential integration of AI with other emerging technologies in real estate investing. Cover areas such as blockchain for secure transactions, IoT for smart property management, and augmented reality (AR) for innovative property showings.

- Discuss how these integrations could offer more transparent, efficient, and engaging real estate investment experiences.

11.10.3 Personalization at Scale

- Delve into the future possibilities of AI in providing personalized investment advice and services at scale. Explain how AI could tailor investment strategies to individual investor profiles, taking into account personal preferences, risk tolerance, and financial goals.

11.10.4 AI in Sustainable and Smart Real Estate Development

- Discuss the role of AI in promoting sustainable and smart real estate development. Highlight how AI could assist in designing energy-efficient buildings, optimizing resource use, and contributing to sustainable urban planning.

11.10.5 Enhanced Decision-Making in Real Estate Investment

- Project how AI advancements could further enhance decision-making in real estate investment. Cover aspects such as AI-driven risk assessment models, market entry timing, and portfolio diversification strategies.

11.10.6 Ethical and Regulatory Evolution

- Address the future ethical and regulatory landscape for AI in real estate investing. Speculate on how laws and ethical guidelines might evolve to keep pace with AI advancements, ensuring responsible use of AI in real estate.

11.10.7 Preparing for an AI-Driven Future in Real Estate

- Conclude by advising real estate professionals and investors on how to prepare for an AI-driven future. Emphasize the importance of staying informed about AI trends, adapting to new technologies, and investing in AI literacy and skills development.

Conclusion The future of AI in real estate investing holds immense promise, with advancements in AI technology set to further transform how properties are marketed, managed, and invested in. As AI continues to evolve, its integration into real estate investing will likely offer unprecedented efficiencies, insights, and opportunities, shaping the industry in profound ways.

Appendix

The Appendix of your book serves as a valuable resource for readers who wish to delve deeper into the topics covered. It can include additional information, resources, and tools that complement the main content of the book.

A. Resources for AI Learning and Development

- **A.1 Comprehensive List of AI Educational Resources:** Provide a curated list of books, online courses, websites, and tutorials that offer foundational and advanced knowledge in AI and machine learning.

- **A.2 Directory of AI Tools and Software:** Include a list of AI tools and software, including GPT-4 and related technologies, with descriptions and links to their respective websites or platforms.

- **A.3 AI Communities and Forums:** List online communities, forums, and groups where readers can engage with AI professionals, enthusiasts, and learners for knowledge sharing and networking.

B. Glossary of AI Terms

- **B.1 Key AI and Real Estate Terminology:** Offer a glossary of key AI and real estate terms used throughout the book, providing clear and concise definitions to aid reader understanding.

- **B.2 Acronyms and Abbreviations:** Include a section for acronyms and abbreviations related to AI and real estate investing for quick reference.

C. Case Study References and Sources

- **C.1 Detailed References for Case Studies:** Provide full references and sources for the case studies included in the book, allowing readers to explore these examples in greater depth.

- **C.2 Additional Case Studies and Examples:** Include additional case studies and real-world examples that offer further insights into the application of AI in real estate.

D. AI Ethics Guidelines and Frameworks

- **D.1 Overview of AI Ethics Principles:** Present a summary of key AI ethics principles and frameworks relevant to real estate investing.

- **D.2 Resources for Staying Informed on AI Ethics:** List resources such as organizations, publications, and conferences focused on AI ethics, particularly in the context of real estate.

E. Updates and Future Trends

- **E.1 Keeping Up with AI Advancements:** Provide advice and resources on how to stay updated with ongoing advancements and future trends in AI and real estate technology.

- **E.2 Predictions and Speculations:** Include a section on predictions and speculations about the future of AI in real estate, based on current trends and technological advancements.

F. About the Author

- **F.1 Author's Biography:** Provide a brief biography of the author, highlighting your expertise and experience in AI and real estate.

- **F.2 Contact Information:** Include contact information or social media handles for readers to connect with the author for further engagement or inquiries.

Index

- **Comprehensive Index:** A thorough index of topics, names, and key terms used in the book for easy reference and navigation.

Resources for AI Learning and Development

This section provides a comprehensive list of resources for readers interested in deepening their understanding of AI and its applications, especially in real estate. These resources range from online courses and books to forums and tools, catering to a variety of learning styles and expertise levels.

A.1 Online Courses and Educational Platforms

- **AI and Machine Learning Courses:** List top online courses and platforms offering AI and machine learning education, such as Coursera, edX, and Udacity. Include courses from beginner to advanced levels, covering topics from basic AI concepts to specialized applications in real estate.

- **GPT-4 Specific Learning Materials:** Provide resources and tutorials specifically focused on GPT-4, including OpenAI's documentation and online communities discussing its latest developments.

A.2 Books and Publications

- **Introductory and Advanced AI Books:** Suggest a range of books that cover AI fundamentals and advanced topics. Include titles that are accessible to beginners as well as those offering in-depth analysis for more experienced readers.

- **Real Estate Technology Publications:** Recommend books and publications that focus on the intersection of AI and real estate, offering insights into current trends and future predictions.

A.3 Online Forums and Communities

- **AI Discussion Forums:** Provide a list of online forums and communities where enthusiasts and professionals discuss AI trends, challenges, and advancements. Include platforms like Reddit, Stack Overflow, and LinkedIn groups.

- **Real Estate Technology Networks:** List online networks and communities where real estate professionals discuss the integration of technology, including AI, in their field. These can be great places for networking and sharing knowledge.

A.4 Tools and Software for AI Development

- **AI Development Tools:** Offer a list of tools and software commonly used in AI development, such as TensorFlow, PyTorch, and Jupyter Notebooks. Include resources for both beginners and advanced developers.

- **Real Estate Specific AI Tools:** Highlight AI tools and platforms that are specifically designed for real estate applications, such as predictive analytics software, market analysis tools, and property valuation models.

A.5 Workshops, Seminars, and Conferences

- **AI and Real Estate Conferences:** Provide information on notable workshops, seminars, and conferences focused on AI and real estate. These events are opportunities for learning from experts and networking with peers.

A.6 Podcasts and Webinars

- **Educational Podcasts and Webinars:** Suggest a selection of podcasts and webinars that focus on AI and its applications in various sectors, including real estate. These can offer convenient and insightful learning experiences.

Glossary of AI Terms

This glossary provides definitions for key terms related to Artificial Intelligence (AI), particularly those mentioned throughout the book. It serves as a quick reference to help readers familiarize themselves with AI terminology, especially as it relates to real estate.

Algorithm: A set of rules or instructions given to an AI program to help it learn and make decisions.

Artificial Intelligence (AI): The simulation of human intelligence processes by machines, especially computer systems. These processes include learning, reasoning, self-correction, and more.

Big Data: Extremely large data sets that may be analyzed computationally to reveal patterns, trends, and associations, especially relating to human behavior and interactions.

Chatbot: A computer program designed to simulate conversation with human users, especially over the Internet.

Data Mining: The practice of examining large databases to generate new information and identify patterns.

Deep Learning: A subset of machine learning involving neural networks with many layers. It enables the model to learn and make intelligent decisions on its own.

GPT-4 (Generative Pre-trained Transformer 4): An advanced version of the AI language model developed by OpenAI, capable of understanding and generating human-like text based on the input it receives.

Machine Learning: A type of AI that allows software applications to become more accurate at predicting outcomes without being explicitly programmed to do so.

Natural Language Processing (NLP): A field of AI that gives machines the ability to read, understand, and derive meaning from human languages.

Neural Network: A series of algorithms that endeavor to recognize underlying relationships in a set of data through a process that mimics the way the human brain operates.

Predictive Analytics: The use of data, statistical algorithms, and machine learning techniques to identify the likelihood of future outcomes based on historical data.

ROI (Return on Investment): A measure used to evaluate the efficiency or profitability of an investment.

Smart Contracts: Self-executing contracts with the terms of the agreement between buyer and seller being directly written into lines of code.

Supervised Learning: A type of machine learning where the model is trained on a labeled dataset, meaning the model is learning from examples that already contain the answers.

Unsupervised Learning: A type of machine learning that uses algorithms to analyze and cluster unlabeled datasets. These algorithms discover hidden patterns or data groupings without the need for human intervention.

About the Author

Ernie Braveboy is a recognized expert in the fields of Artificial Intelligence (AI) and real estate investment. With over two decades of experience, Ernie has dedicated his career to exploring the transformative potential of AI in various industries, particularly in real estate.

Ernie's passion for AI and its applications was ignited during his early career in software development. As he witnessed the rapid advancements in AI technology, he recognized its potential to revolutionize traditional business models and create new opportunities for income generation.

Throughout his career, Ernie has been at the forefront of AI innovation, working with cutting-edge technologies and staying up-to-date with the latest developments. His expertise spans a wide range of AI applications, from natural language processing and predictive analytics to deep learning and chatbot development.

Ernie is not only a technical expert but also a visionary strategist. He has successfully integrated AI into real estate investment strategies, enabling more informed decision-making, predictive modeling, and personalized customer experiences. His insights and hands-on experience have allowed him to achieve remarkable success in the real estate industry.

In addition to his practical experience, Ernie is a passionate educator. He has conducted workshops, webinars, and training sessions to empower others to harness the power of AI for income generation. His ability to demystify complex AI concepts and make them accessible to a broader audience has earned him a reputation as an engaging and knowledgeable speaker.

Ernie Braveboy's commitment to responsible AI use, ethical considerations, and the future of AI technology in various industries is evident in his work. He believes in the potential of AI to create a positive impact on society while ensuring that it aligns with ethical principles and legal regulations.

As the author of "The GPT-4 Advantage: Unlocking the Secrets of AI-Driven Income," Ernie shares his expertise, insights, and practical guidance with readers, offering a roadmap to leverage AI, particularly GPT-4, for income generation in the dynamic world of real estate investing.

Ernie Braveboy invites readers to connect with him through his website, social media, or professional network to continue the conversation on AI and real estate and to stay informed about the latest developments in the field.

Conclusion

In the journey through the pages of "The GPT-4 Advantage: Unlocking the Secrets of AI-Driven Income," we've embarked on an exploration of the incredible potential of Artificial Intelligence, specifically GPT-4, to revolutionize the landscape of income generation, with a primary focus on real estate investing. We've delved into the intricacies of AI technology, uncovered innovative money-making ideas, and navigated the ethical considerations that arise in this rapidly evolving field.

As we reach the conclusion of this book, it's essential to reflect on the knowledge and insights you've gained. The world of AI is dynamic, and its applications continue to expand, offering limitless opportunities for those who embrace its capabilities. The fusion of AI and real estate has unlocked new dimensions of predictive analytics, personalized customer experiences, and efficient decision-making, presenting you with the tools to thrive in this ever-changing landscape.

I hope the book was able to help you fill in the blank with innovative ideas, strategies, and the confidence to harness the power of AI in your real estate ventures. Your journey toward AI-driven income is just beginning, and the possibilities are boundless.

Remember that the future is yours to shape, and with the knowledge gained from this book, you are well-equipped to stay at the forefront of AI advancements and leverage them for your financial success. Keep exploring, learning, and applying the principles discussed here to unlock the secrets of AI-driven income in your real estate endeavors.

Thank you for embarking on this journey with me, and I wish you unparalleled success in your AI-driven ventures. The future is bright, and you have the power to seize it.

Finally, if you enjoyed this book, then I'd like to ask you for a favor, would you be kind enough to leave a review for this book on Amazon? It'd be greatly appreciated!

Thank you and good luck!

The Landlord's Playbook -PART 2- : Mastering Section 8 Rentals for Maximum Cash Flow

As a Section 8 landlord, your journey doesn't have to stop with a single rental property. Scaling your rental business allows you to expand your portfolio, increase your rental income, and achieve greater financial success. In this chapter, we'll explore strategies and considerations for scaling your Section 8 rental business effectively and sustainably.

Section 1: Acquiring New Properties

Expanding your rental portfolio begins with acquiring new properties. Here are some key steps and considerations:

- Market Research: Conduct thorough market research to identify areas with strong demand for Section 8 rentals and potential for growth.

- Financing Options: Explore financing options such as mortgages, loans, or partnerships to fund property acquisitions.

- Property Selection: Choose properties that align with the Section 8 program's requirements and have the potential for positive cash flow.

Section 2: Financing Growth

Scaling your rental business often requires financial resources. Consider these strategies for financing your expansion:

- Leverage Existing Equity: If you own properties with equity, consider tapping into that equity to fund new acquisitions.

- Partnerships: Explore partnerships with investors or real estate professionals who can provide capital and expertise.

148

- Real Estate Financing: Work with lenders who specialize in real estate financing to secure favorable terms and rates.

Section 3: Diversifying Investments

Diversification can reduce risk and enhance your rental business's stability:

- o **Property Types:** Consider diversifying your property types to include single-family homes, multi-unit buildings, or different housing markets.

- **Geographic Diversity:** Expanding into different geographic areas can help mitigate market-specific risks.

- **Income Streams:** Explore additional income streams within the real estate industry, such as short-term rentals or property management services.

Section 4: Property Management Systems

Efficient property management is essential when scaling your rental business:

- **Streamlining Operations:** Implement property management systems and software to streamline tasks such as rent collection, maintenance, and tenant communication.

- **Leveraging Technology:** Embrace technology for marketing, tenant screening, and property maintenance.

- **Outsourcing and Delegation:** Consider outsourcing tasks such as property maintenance or hiring property managers to handle day-to-day operations.

Section 5: Long-Term Planning

Scaling your rental business is a long-term endeavor. Develop a comprehensive plan.

CHECK OUT MY OTHER BOOKS

Below you'll find some of my other popular books that are popular on Amazon and Kindle as well. Simply click on the links below to check them out. Alternatively, you can visit my author page on Amazon to see other work done by me.

How to Make Huge Cash with Section 8 Rentals - THE LANDLORD HANDBOOK

https:/ /www.amazon.com/Make-Section-Rentals- Landlord-Handbook-ebook/dp/B0757ZFRZZ?ref_=ast_sto_dp

How to Deal With Debt Collectors and Win Every Time - How to Beat Them at Their Own Game

https:/ /www.amazon.com/Deal-Debt-Collectors-Every-Their-ebook/dp/B07CSW9GDV?ref_=ast_sto_dp

First Time Home Buyers Guide - Everything You Need to Know Before Buying Your First House

https:/ /www.amazon.com/First-Time-Home-Buyers-Guide-ebook/dp/B08DRDL22Z?ref_=ast_sto_dp

How Small Investors Can Get Started In Commercial Properties - A Beginner Guide to Buying Your First Commercial Property

https://www.amazon.com/INVESTORS-COMMERCIAL-
PROPERTIES-Beginner-Commercial-

ebook/dp/B07DLP2T6Q ?ref_=ast_sto_dp

Real Estate Marketing- How to Be a Real-Estate Millionaire

https:/   /www.amazon.com/REAL-ESTATE-MARKETING-REAL-
ESTATE-MILLIONAIRE-ebook/dp/B077SWRRRC?ref_=ast_sto_dp

How to Make Your First Million Dollars With Airbnb - A Beginner
Guide to Make Huge Cash With Airbnb

https:/   /www.amazon.com/Make-First-Million-Dollars-Airbnb-
ebook/dp/B0825MG7VC?ref_=ast_sto_dp

Your Guide to Financial Freedom - How to Stop Living From
Paycheck to Paycheck

https://www.amazon.com/Guide-Financial-Freedom-Living-
Paycheck-ebook/dp/B07CSRWWWY?ref_=ast_sto_dp

How to Wholesale Houses for Huge Cash - Part II (With Contracts
Included)

https:/ /www.amazon.com/wholesale-more-houses-essential-bundles-
ebook/dp/B07JKJX6P 4?ref_=ast_sto_dp

Credit Repair - How to Repair Your Credit All By Yourself - A
Beginners Guide to Better Credit

https:/ /www.amazon.com/Credit-Repair-Yourself-Beginners-Better-ebook/dp/B07CW41SJK?ref_ =ast_sto_dp

How to Wholesale Houses for Huge Cash + How to Wholesale Houses for Huge Cash- Part 2

https:/ /www.amazon.com/wholesale-your-first-house-little-ebook/dp/B07DBVBD 1T?ref_=ast_sto_dp

You Guide to Financial Freedom - How to Stop Living From Paycheck to Paycheck + Credit Repair - How to Repair Your Credit All by Yourself

https:/ /www.amazon.com/number-guide-credit-financial-freedom-ebook/dp/B07DLKNKZX?ref_=ast_sto_dp

How to Deal With Debt Collectors and Win Every Time How to Beat Them at Their Own Game + Credit Repair: How to Repair Your Credit All By Yourself

https:/ /www.amazon.com/beginner-guide-collectors-credit-fast-ebook/dp/B07DL1DTP6?ref_ =ast_sto_dp

Real Estate Marketing - How to be a Real-Estate Millionaire + How You too can be successful and Make Lots of Money Even If You Have No Talent + How Small Investors Can Get Started In Commercial Properties + How to Buy, Fix and Sell Your Property and Make a Ton of Money

https:/ /www.amazon.com/complete-real-estate-investor-guide-ebook/dp/B07DHFW4SL?ref_=ast_sto_dp

How to Wholesale Houses for Huge Cash + How to Wholesale Houses for Huge Cash Part II+ Real Estate Marketing

https://www.amazon.com/learn-wholesale-houses-everything-guide-ebook/dp/B07DD7BZY1?ref_=ast_sto_dp

How Small Investors Can Get Started in Commercial Properties - A Beginner Guide to Buying Your First Commercial Property

https:/ /www.amazon.com/Investors-Commercial-Properties-Beginner-Property-ebook/dp/B07BD2 JDCC?ref_=ast_sto_dp

How to Wholesale Houses for Huge Profits

https:/ /www.amazon.com/how-wholesale-houses-huge-profit-ebook/dp/B0714GRHTB?ref_=ast_sto_dp

How to Wholesale Houses for Huge Cash - Part II

https:/ /www.amazon.com/WHOLESALE-H OUSES-HUGE-CONTRACTS-INCLUDED-ebook/ dp/B0791LFSYD?ref_=ast_sto_dp

How to Buy, Fix and Sell Your Property and Make a Ton of Money

https:/ /www.amazon.com/Sell-Your-Property-Make-Money-ebook/dp/B0755HS4LT?ref_=ast_sto_dp

How To Be a Great Landlord - Make Huge Profit and Make Your Tenants Love You https:/ /www.amazon.com/Great-Landlord-Make-Profit-Tenants-ebook/dp/B071YX9L3Y?ref_=ast_sto_dp

I Can't Breathe: Living While Black In America - The Ultimate Death Sentence

https:/ /www.amazon.com/Cant-Breathe-America-Ultimate-Sentence-ebook/dp/B08FGCY2Vl ?ref_=ast_sto_dp

Legal Cannabis Will be Bigger Than Cryptos - A Beginner Guide to CBD Investing

https:/ /www.amazon.com/Cannabis- Bigger-Cryptos-Beginner-Investing-ebook/dp/B07WVYJJ8J?ref_=ast_sto_dp

How to Make Your First Million Dollars with Airbnb: A Beginner Guide to Make Huge Cash with Airbnb

https:/ /www.amazon.com/Make-First-Million-Dollars-Airbnb-ebook/dp/B0825MG7VC?ref_=ast_sto_dp

YouTube Channel Success: How to Create a Great YouTube Channel, Gain Millions of Subscribers, and Make Money Too

https://www.amazon.com/YOUTUBE-CHANNEL-SUCCESS-MILLIONSOF-SUBSCRIBERS-

ebook/dp/B07GX8YTCH?ref_=ast_sto_dp

FROM STARTUP TO SUCCESS: A Guide to LLC & S-Corp

Formation and Taxation https://a.co/ d/cXJ59Pk

The Autism-Friendly Cookbook: No-Sugar, Low-Carb Recipes for Picky Eaters

https://a.co/d/0so33q8

FIX IT YOURSELF: A STEP-BY-STEP GUIDE TO HOME PLUMBING REPAIRS

https://a.co/d/gitXlY4

The Ultimate Weight Loss Hack:: How to Lose 50 Pounds in Just 30 Days Without Starving Yourself

https://a.co/d/5GneTeM

The Science of Sleep : A book that delves into the latest research on sleep and offers practical advice for getting better quality

https://a.co/d/4ThXX2Y

Stock Investing for Beginners in 2023: Maximizing Your Investment Potential: A Guide for New Investors in the Post COVID-19 Economy

https://a.co/ d/hF2S42Z

The Homeowner's Guide to Heating and Air Conditioning : 10 Essential Tips for Maintaining Your Heating and Air Conditioning Unit

https://a.co/d/ecT7Evs

If the links do not work, for whatever reason, you can simply search for these titles on the Amazon website to find them.

www.ingramcontent.com/pod-product-compliance
Lightning Source LLC
LaVergne TN
LVHW052101060326
832903LV00060B/2468